THE ART OF
CHINESE FLOWER ARRANGEMENT

www.royalcollins.com

THE ART OF

CHINESE FLOWER ARRANGEMENT

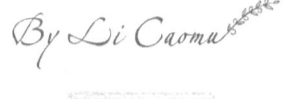

By Li Caomu

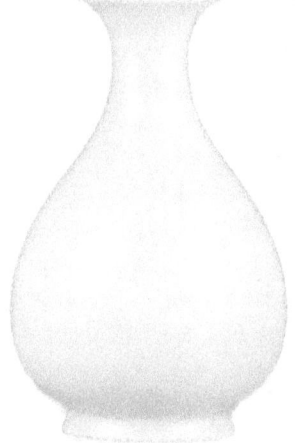

RC

Books Beyond Boundaries

ROYAL COLLINS

The Art of Chinese Flower Arrangement

Li Caomu

First English Edition 2020
By Royal Collins Publishing Group Inc.
BKM ROYALCOLLINS PUBLISHERS PRIVATE LIMITED
www.royalcollins.com

Headquarters: 550-555 boul. René-Lévesque O Montréal (Québec) H2Z1B1 Canada
India office: 805 Hemkunt House, 8th Floor, Rajendra Place, New Delhi 110 008

ISBN: 978-1-4878-0369-8

PREFACE

This book was inspired by my passion for the art of Chinese flower arranging. The arrangement of flowers is an important component of a refined Chinese lifestyle, and is practiced in various forms such as interior decoration, the cultivation of taste, and the development of sensory acuity. In recent years, this refined lifestyle has reappeared, with increasing interest in piano playing, chess, books, paintings, poetry, wine, flowers, tea, and songs. Among these elements, flowers are the most obvious embodiment of the relationship between humans and nature. As a means of expression, the flower is also highly inclusive and strongly adaptable. For me, flowers are a medium to explore the world, to appreciate its vastness, and to inspire an awareness and understanding of life.

As the originator of the art form in the East, China has a long history of flower arranging and the mental cultivation methods that go along with it. It is an all-encompassing discipline that also includes the country's bronze and porcelain cultures, as well as its calligraphy, songs, poetry, and ethics. Against relevant cultural backgrounds, it uses aesthetics as the basis and flowers as the materials to recreate the beauty of life. However, many students of flower arranging today have deviated from the authentic learning and practice of its culture. As Confucius wrote, "to learn without thinking is blindness; to think without learning is idleness", therefore a fresh wave of self-reflection is clearly required.

The book begins with an overview of relevant Chinese culture, determining the direction of research for Chinese flower arranging. It combines aesthetics with commonly used designs, enabling students to create products that embody both the material form and the inner spirit of the arrangements. Masterpieces can be created from arranging flowers. In the process, practitioners can develop their personal aesthetics, leading to the formation of healthy living habits and improving the quality of life.

This book also contains visual references for students, based on related cultural and aesthetic knowledge. With their attractive appearance, distinct styles, and flexible requirements for the branches and shapes of flowers, these examples cleverly harness the essence of nature. In emulating them, students will be able to broaden their horizons and develop their creativity.

The book covers a wide range of areas, reflecting the comprehensiveness of Chinese flower arranging. With content that is easy to follow, its aim is to broaden training in this area and inspire more students to co-create a robust future for the art form. During the writing process, I have received generous assistance from Chen Xiaojiu, Huang Chunxiao, Zhang Xiruo, Lu Dongying, Long Huan, and other friends and family members, and would like to use this opportunity to express my heartfelt thanks.

Li Caomu
16th October 2016

ABOUT THE AUTHOR

Li Caomu – the founder of *Caomu Huadao* – is a professional flower arranger and a veteran of landscape design. Born on 13th December 1981 in Quanjiao Country, Anhui Province, he is an avid fan of Chinese paintings, and has been painting for many years. After graduating from the Fine Arts Department at Wuhu Teachers College in 2002, he began to work in floral and landscape design, which gave him a solid foundation in natural aesthetics. During the course of his studies of Chinese flower art and ancient methods, he learned to incorporate best practices from both China and abroad into his work. As well as launching *Caomu Huadao*, he has established modern principles for flower arranging based on aesthetic theories, bringing the art of Chinese flower arranging into daily life.

Li is the author of China's first contemporary book about flower arranging, titled "Techniques for Hand-Drawing Flower Arrangements". He has published a wide range of papers, creating a far-reaching and lasting impact for his design concepts. He is also the author of the stage drama "Weeping Flowers", which deals with the process of flower arranging. Setting a precedent for performances of this genre, the work covers flower arrangements that are influenced by landscape aesthetics. Such arrangements possess defining characteristics and profound meanings, as well as styles that are subtle, concise, and well-blended.

Li Caomu's work has enabled the art of Chinese flower arranging to remain rooted in tradition while preserving its modernity.

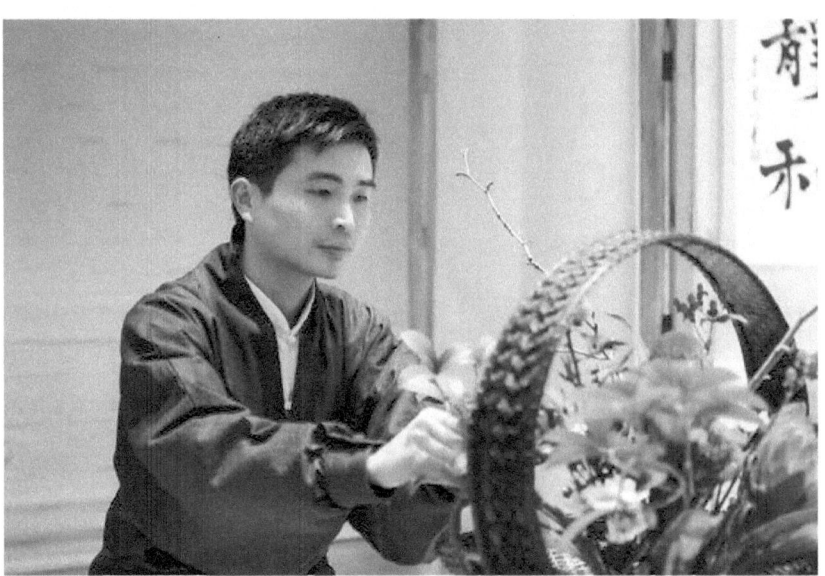

CONTENTS

CONTENTS

1

An Overview of Chinese Flower Arranging

1. Introduction

Flower arranging is an applied discipline that combines practicality and art. A vehicle for the cultivation of taste, it also enables the practitioner to acquire related historical and cultural information and aesthetic knowledge. Well-arranged flowers will beautify the space used by enhancing the atmosphere and improving the occupants' mood. The arranging process will also emphasize the metaphorical meaning of the flowers and products, and can strengthen interpersonal bonds through the conveying of good wishes accompanied by gifts. In recent years, flowers and flower arrangements have become fashionable for a generation seeking modern, refined lifestyles – a good example of the art form's life-enhancing potential.

2. The Development of Chinese Flower Arranging

The art of Chinese flower arranging is considered as one of the nation's cultural treasures. Flowers are naturally attractive, and humans are born with the tendency to seek good things for a better life. Throughout history, people have decorated porcelain with beautiful floral designs. Ancient societies adorned their pottery and bronzes in the same way. Around 3,000 years ago during the Spring and Autumn Period (771-476 BC),, the earliest poetry collection – *The Book of Songs: Zhengfeng and Qinwei River* – records a description of young men and women expressing their affection through the exchange of flowers known as 'classical twists'. During the Warring States Period (475–221 BC),, the poet Qu Yuan's poem 'Li Sao' includes a description of flowers being plucked to wear as an accessory. Flowers were used for personal decoration, for the expression of emotions, and for the stating of intent, imbuing them with various levels of meaning. This laid the foundation for the art of flower arranging.

According to historical records, the planting of flowers in containers in China was first practiced during the Six Dynasties Period (AD 222–589). Around 1,500 years ago, the *Southern History* recorded the offering of flowers to Buddha for the purpose of curing ailments. The earliest artefact related to flower arranging is a statue of Guanyin, Goddess of Mercy, from the Northern Zhou Dynasty (AD 557–581), which is currently exhibited at London's Victoria and Albert Museum. The statue holds a vase of flowers, with perfect proportions between the foliage and the vessel. This reflects the high status of flowers in ancient times, and proves their importance in daily life.

Flower arranging flourished during the Sui and Tang Dynasties (AD 580–907), with the organizing of the annual Hundred Flowers Festival in February. 'The Nine Elements Given to Renowned Flowers', written by Luo Qiu during the Tang Dynasty (AD 618–907), recorded normative procedures and aesthetics of the art, indicating its prevalence in the lives of the upper classes and literati. Artificial flowers were also widely used during this period. The earliest known specimen of such flowers was a bouquet unearthed in Astana, southeast of Turpan in Xinjiang, which displayed bright, realistic colors and high-quality workmanship. China was rich and powerful during this period, and the art form spread quickly within the country and beyond.

During the Five Dynasties and Ten Kingdoms Period (AD 907–960), political turmoil led the literati to flee and live in seclusion. Flower arranging became a way for them to express their thoughts and feelings. Their style changed from reflecting solemnness to simplicity, with the use of wild flowers and weeds, and many types of container. During the same period, Guo Jiangzhou invented a special flower arranging vessel known as *zhanjing pan* for the same purpose. In the Southern Tang Dynasty (AD 937–976), the ruler Li Yu made a significant contribution to the field with the creation of the *jin dong tian* – a large-scale displaying device.

Flower arranging reached its peak during the Song Dynasty (AD 960–1279). In those days it was practiced for pleasure and entertainment, while also conveying rational ideas, philosophy, and morals. Flowers that carried deep metaphorical meanings (such as pine, cypress, bamboo, plum, orchid, cassia, camellia, and narcissus) were chosen to reflect moral character. The composition involved fine lines as a rule of thumb, with styles that were clean and elegant, followed by the use of flowers as symbols. This had a lasting impact on future generations. Flower baskets from the Song Dynasty emphasize both the naturalness and metaphorical meanings of the blooms. For instance, Li Song's examples from the Southern Song Dynasty (1127–1279) feature exquisite exteriors, with lush but delicate floral patterns including half-open or blossoming hemerocallis, pomegranate, peony, and hollyhock.

The influence of Neo-Confucianism had faded by the Yuan Dynasty (1271–1368), with metaphorical meanings and homophones being used to express the themes. Renowned artist Qian Xuanhui created basket-style flower arrangements by taking two porcelain vases decorated with osmanthus branches, and filling them with osmanthus flowers to signify prosperity. This arrangement reflected a desire for freedom and peace.

The art reached maturity in the Ming Dynasty (1368–1644), when the techniques and theories came to form a complete system. Many works were influenced by Song Dynasty aesthetics, and were designed for the main hall, such as Bian Weijin's 'Comprehensive

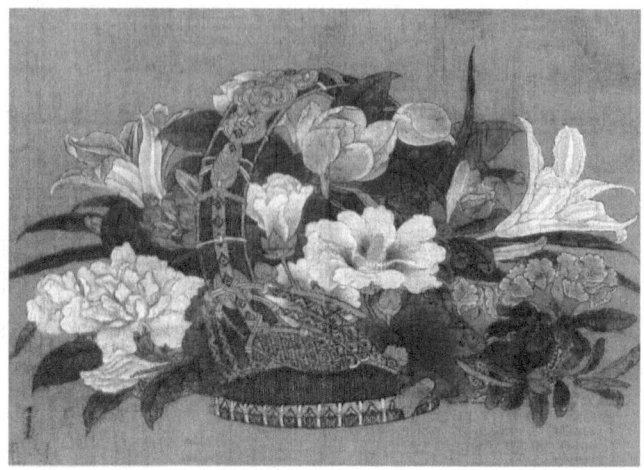

Li Song - 'Images of a Flower Basket' **(Song Dynasty, AD 960-1279)**

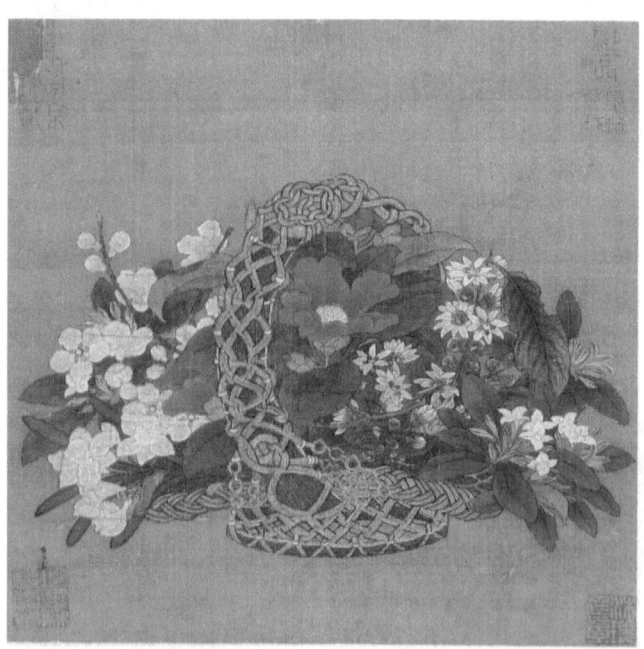

Li Song - 'Images of a Flower Basket' **(Song Dynasty, AD 960-1279)**

Bottled Flowers for the Hall'. Imbued with rich symbolism, these works implied the beauty of completeness, with each flower possessing a different meaning. Towards the middle of the Ming Dynasty, people began to favor simplicity and often used *ganoderma* and coral along with flowers. In the later years of the dynasty there was a turn towards naturalness across all art forms. This period also witnessed the maturity of artistic theory and the publication of much related literature.

This literature included Zhang Qiande's *Bottled Flowers Manual* and Yuan Hongdao's *History of Bottles*, which were particularly influential in terms of composition, flower plucking, maintenance, grading, and display vessels. They also contained important information about configurations, the environment, cultivation, and appreciation, as well theories and techniques. Publications by Jin Run, Gao Lian, He Xianlang, Tu Benjun, and Wen Zhengheng included in-depth research into the processing, maintenance, composition, color, dimensions, and appeal of flowers. The formation of these theories is of great significance to the development and legacy of the art.

In the early Qing Dynasty (1644–1911), flower arranging was influenced by bonsai landscaping, which advocated natural beauty. This was seen in Zou Yigui's scenery-related arrangements, in which bamboo and palm were combined with Taihu stone. Homophonic flower arrangements were also popular, with the first Chinese character of every flower's name used to form a collective term. Li Yu's *Leisure Collections* and Shen Fu's *Leisure Records* detailed the natural imagery and strategy of the art, which led to a fresh wave of rapid development. However, flower arranging gradually faded out due to the political turmoil of the late Qing Dynasty.

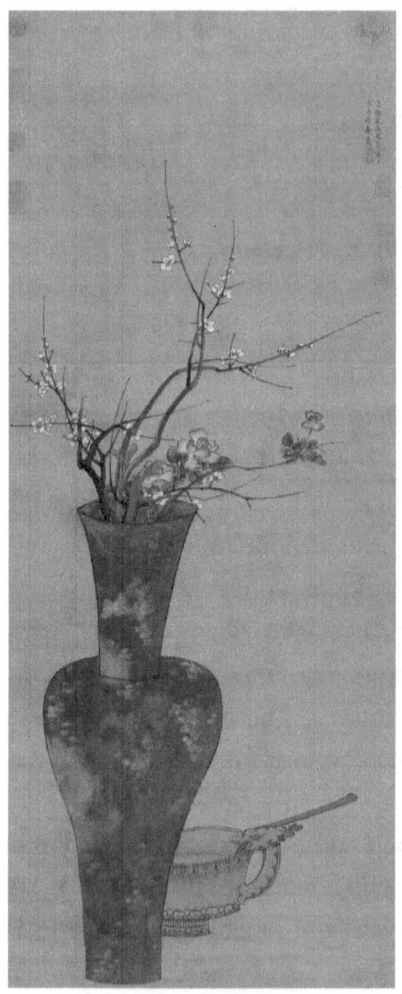

Chen Hongshou - 'Images of Bright
Offerings and Artefacts'
(Ming Dynasty, 1368-1644)

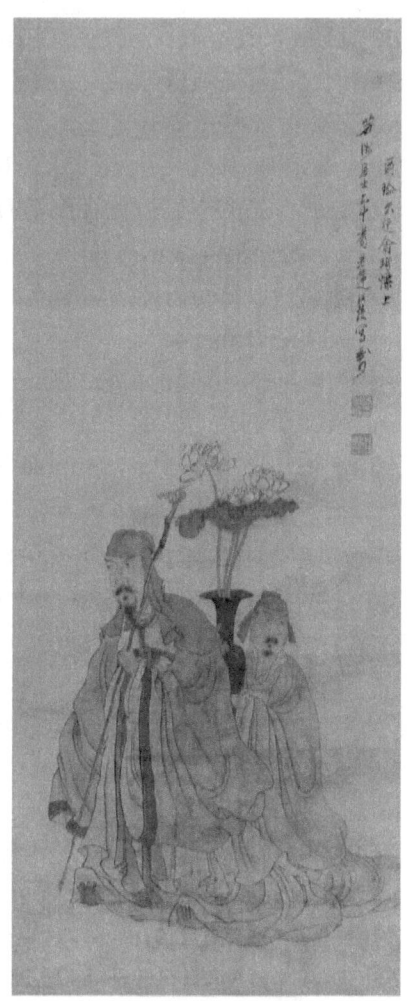

Chen Hongshou - 'A Hermit
Holding a Lotus'
(Ming Dynasty, 1368-1644)

From the establishment of the new People's Republic of China (1949), through Reform and Opening Up (beginning 1978), and with the development of the horticultural industry, flower arranging has undergone a long process of recovery. Regions such as Beijing, Guangzhou, and Shanghai began to set up localized flower arranging associations. Today, exhibitions and events are organized nationwide, promoting the art and boosting its popularity. To maintain high

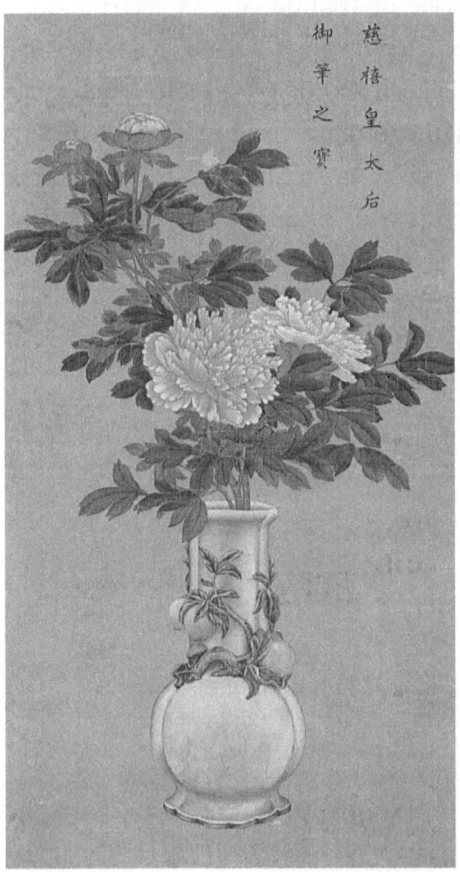

Empress Dowager Cixi – 'Mirror Heart' **(Qing Dynasty, 1644-1911)**

standards, flower arranging courses are conducted, often in high schools. With the integrated development of Eastern and Western cultures, practitioners must shoulder the heavy responsibility of continuing and developing this important aspect of China's cultural heritage.

3. The Art of *Caomuhua*

Caomuha is a style of traditional flower arranging that integrates modern aesthetics, replicating Chinese characteristics such as natural and artistic beauty with an emphasis on shape, color and meaning. "Shape" should incorporate the beauty of nature, with a concise design and close attention to lines; "color" should combine elegance and contrast, while the "meaning" should reflect the positive side of human nature, in perfect balance with nature. *Caomuha* can be woven into design concepts and performances, helping to highlight the beauty of the art form.

2

THE DESIGN
AND METHODS OF CHINESE
FLOWER ARRANGING

1. Tools and Materials for Flower Arranging

Commonly used tools for flower arranging include scissors, small handsaws and knives, rags, and shelves, as well as tape, wire, and aluminum foil. There are no fixed requirements for the use of tools and processes, as they are dependent on the actual situation, i.e. the nature of the particular plants and environments.

The main tools for Chinese flower arranging are *jianshan* and sponges. A *jianshan* is a display vessel made from copper, tin, or lead. Besides being durable, it can be used for a prolonged period of time and is environmentally friendly. Sponges for fixing the flowers are made using phenol foam. They come in a variety of designs for one-time use. Natural fixation methods can also be used, of which "sa" is the most common. "Sa" refers to the fixed bracket, which is usually shaped like the Chinese characters 一 (one) and 十 (ten).

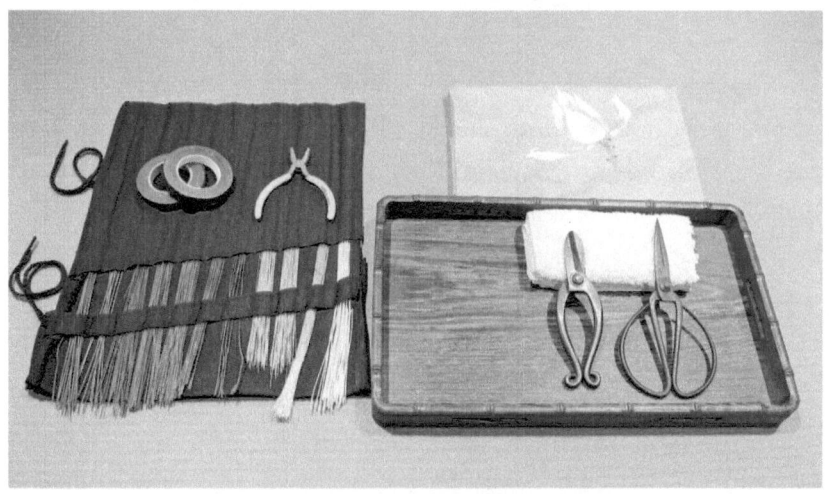

Commonly Used Tools and Materials

– Plugs

A plug is usually used for containers with a wide mouth and shallow body, to create a streamlined design. The flowers are inserted vertically and pushed into the desired position, while overly thick branches are trimmed in an oblique fashion so that they fit. Overly fine flowers are wrapped using tape and gold wires. They can be inserted in either a hidden or an exposed fashion. The parts that are exposed should be neat, but can also be covered using flowers, wood, and gravel, depending on the overall concept.

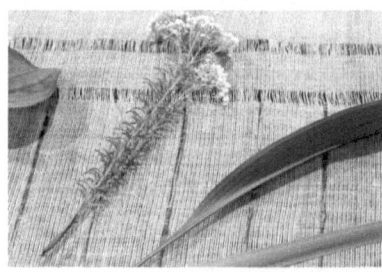 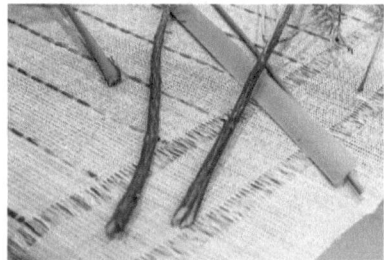

– Sponges

Sponges can be cut into smaller pieces according to requirements, and then placed into water to soak up moisture. The design must include access to the water supply for all of the blooms. A cover can be used to ensure that the stalks are inserted appropriately. Flowers that are placed too shallowly will not reach the water, and may fall out of the display; meanwhile, flowers that are inserted too deeply may become tangled with the other branches, undermining their stability.

– Natural Fixation

The natural fixation method focuses on the aesthetics of the materials while ensuring seamless integration. The '*sa*' fixer should be delicate and stable, both for ease of use and aesthetic appeal.

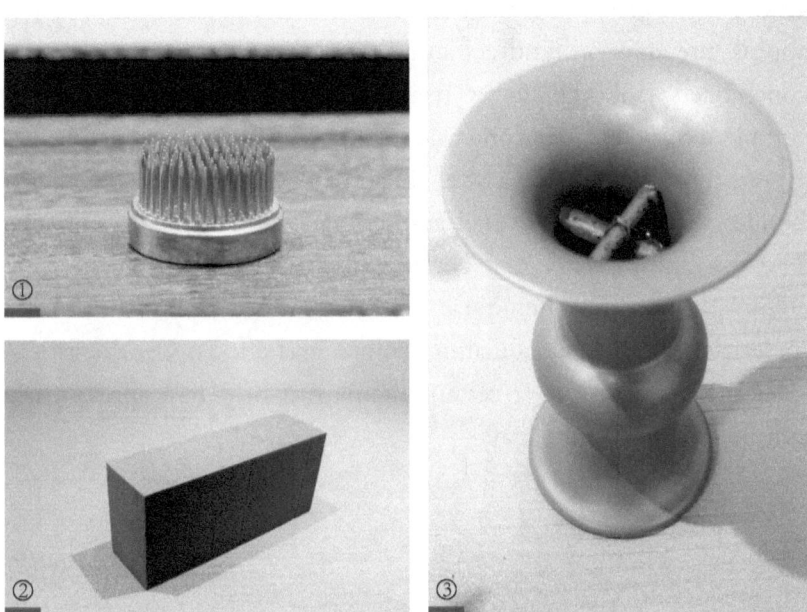

1. Plugs,   2. Sponges,   3. *Sa*

2. Design Concepts for Flower Arranging

Design concepts should be based on the surrounding environment. A typical Chinese environment, be it simple, luxurious, fresh, or static, will reflect certain elements of the local culture. The fundamental element of a design is the sketch, as it provides a rough idea of the designer's ideas, and allows for constant examination and refinement to produce an ideal piece of work. To create works with distinctive features, the design should be based on both aesthetic knowledge and cultural factors. In terms of overall management and details (including flowers, containers, accessories, the environment, and the arrangement process), equal consideration should be given to visual appeal, preservation, and achievability. While the concepts can be concretized while the flower arrangement is in progress, successful completion is dependent on basic aesthetics.

A strong theme adds a vital finishing touch to an arrangement. Besides increasing the overall aesthetic appeal, it helps to enhance a work's cultural value and convey the artist's skill. Under normal circumstances, the theme can be determined from the work's materials, containers, modelling, colors, and effects. On the artists' side, the perfecting of a certain theme can help to improve their cultural literacy.

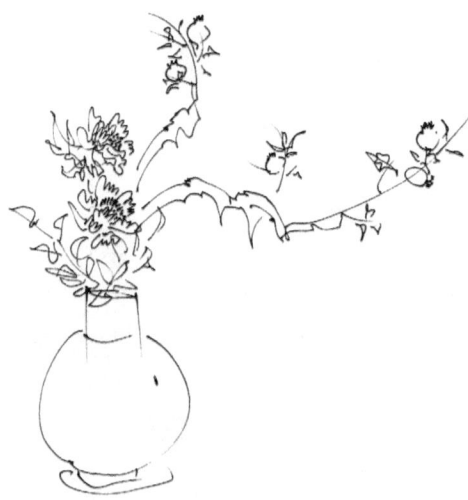

The design concept of floral lines on bottles

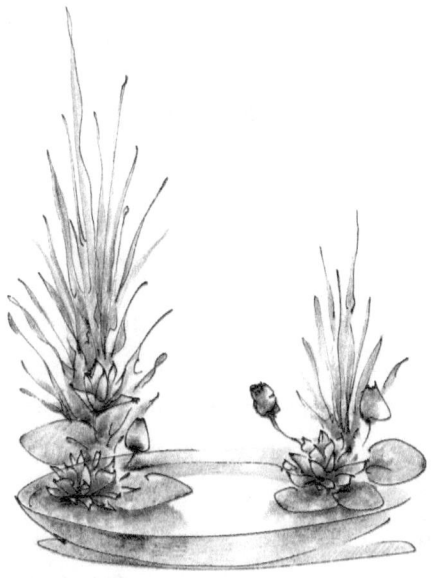

The design concept of flora colors on plates

3. The Process of Flower Arranging

Mastering the steps of flower arranging helps a florist to develop a strong practice. This calls for a consideration of the materials used, as well as external factors such as the surrounding environment and conservation. In normal circumstances, the environment must be designed before choosing the containers and materials, arranging the flowers, cleaning up, and implementing conservation measures. The process usually begins with the insertion of the frame followed by the focus and susceptor, before the other materials are added. During the arrangement process, the materials will form a variety of lines, points, surfaces, and blocks, requiring contrastive analysis to accentuate the distinctive features. When there are limited materials remaining, it is still possible to find suitable reference points to create meaning. As shown below, the appropriate processing of flowers is a necessary part of the practice. However, with excessive processing, flowers risk losing their natural beauty, thus undermining the principles of the art.

– Setting up the Frame

The frame is a major component of a flower arrangement, and forms the basis of the work. The unique characteristics of an arrangement determine how it will be presented. Hence, when inserting the frame, the florist should bear these characteristics in mind, as well as the potential contrasts between the containers and colors. Emphasis should be placed on establishing a space within the main body for the natural growth of the materials. Since the flowers will be distributed in accordance with the frame, this initial step is vital.

– Inserting the Focal Flowers

The focal flowers, usually the largest, are the visual epicenter of an arrangement. Either partially blooming or fully bloomed variants can be selected. The placing of flowers affects the focus of the work, so a holistic approach should be taken to ensure that the focal flowers stand out.

– Arrangements to Complement the Types of Flowers Used

Appropriate complementation will enrich an arrangement and highlight the role of the focal flowers. Relations should be formed, both internally and externally. This can include color, type, and characteristics. Complementary flowers are usually smaller than the focal blooms, adding variety to the arrangement.

— Arrangements to Supplement the Types of Flowers Used
  Supplementary flowers are used to fill gaps in the arrangement,
  enabling improvements to be made throughout the process. This
  results in a final product that is visually complete while preserving
  internal relationships among the flowers.

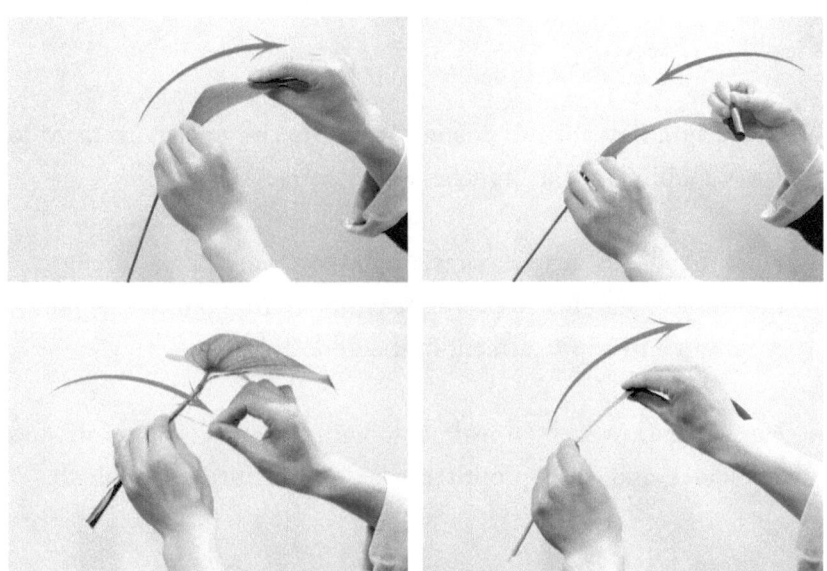

Simple processing of flowers

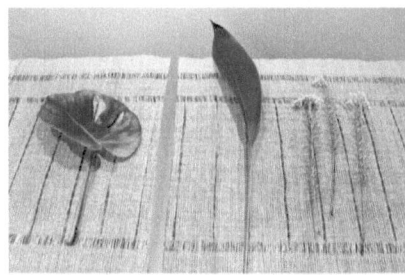

Pre-processing of flowers

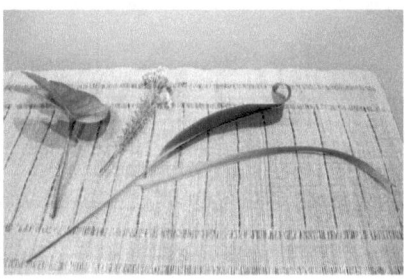

Post-processing of flowers

4. The Maintenance of Flower Arrangements

The maintenance of flower arrangements has a long history. There is a section in *Flower Bottle Records* titled 'Bottle Care', which details the various methods. Likewise, the chapter called 'Washing' in *History of Bottles* has advice on the practice. While flower arrangements are works of art in their own right, they will not last forever. However, with proper care their lifespan can be extended. The following steps should be observed:

— Make sure that there is enough space around an arrangement to allow mobility of the branches and blooms.

— Place the vase in an area that is suitable for fragile items. Strengthen the vessel to stabilize it, paying attention to the connecting points. Apply an anti-slip treatment to the underside.

— Keep the flowers well-hydrated, with plenty of nutrients and pesticides, and the appropriate levels of moisture and sunlight.

3

CREATING
COMMON CHINESE FLOWER
ARRANGEMENTS

There is no strict form of modelling for flower arrangements. Basic designs can be achieved easily by students and beginners. Although man-made, Chinese flower arrangements mirror nature in all its complexity. The secrets that lie within cannot be explained verbally, and must be experienced personally. Hence, this chapter lays out the 'Eight Laws', which involve reflections from first-hand experience.

1. The Eight Laws

– Unity of the Heart and Soul
 Flowers are living entities. Treat them with respect, and you will come to understand their habits and appearances.

– A Clear Distinction Between the Primary and Secondary Aspects
 The appeal of flowers lies in their many facets. A clear distinction between primary and secondary aspects will allow them to display their beauty, order, and clarity across a wider landscape.

– Gathering of Roots and Spreading of Branches
 Gathering roots together makes a plant strong, while the spreading of branches enhances its elegance. This way, flowers can remain rooted while blooming freely.

– Deep Roots with Swaying Branches
 With solid roots and flexible branches, flowers can embody peace of mind.

– The Imaginary Alternating with the Real
When the imaginary is interwoven with the real and vice-versa, both become true.

– Good proportions
A well-proportioned arrangement should resemble a landscape painting, reflecting clear thoughts and a richness of poetic and artistic conception.

– Interaction
Regardless of position, both parties in an interaction should be sincere, thus sharing their individual radiance and beauty.

– Setting the Scene
Flowers are like people; they require a befitting location if they are to flourish. Hence, there should be an emphasis on conveying a flower's meaning when determining its location, taking both internal and external factors into account.

2. Vertically-Arranged Flowers in a Bowl

Name	*Tall and Straight*
Arrangement of Flowers	Vertical
Type of Container	Porcelain bowl engraved with flowers
Types of Flowers	Small purple-red chrysanthemums, alpine, iris leaves, and iron lilies

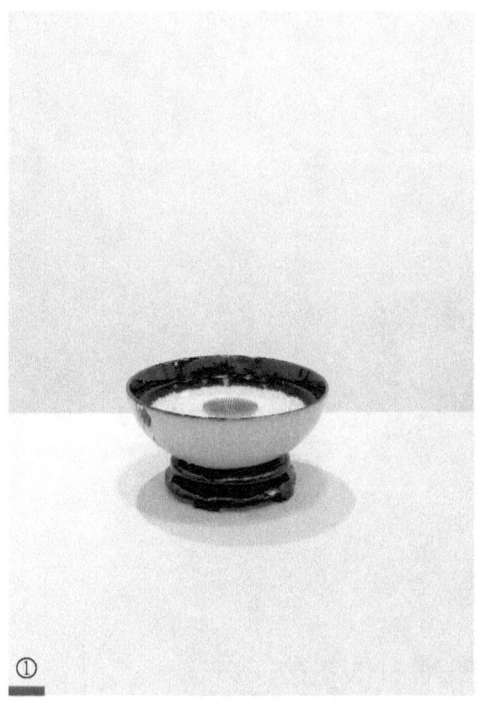

1. Choose an aesthetically pleasing bowl and fill it with gravel to stabilize and elevate the metal fixer within, as well as to increase its mass.

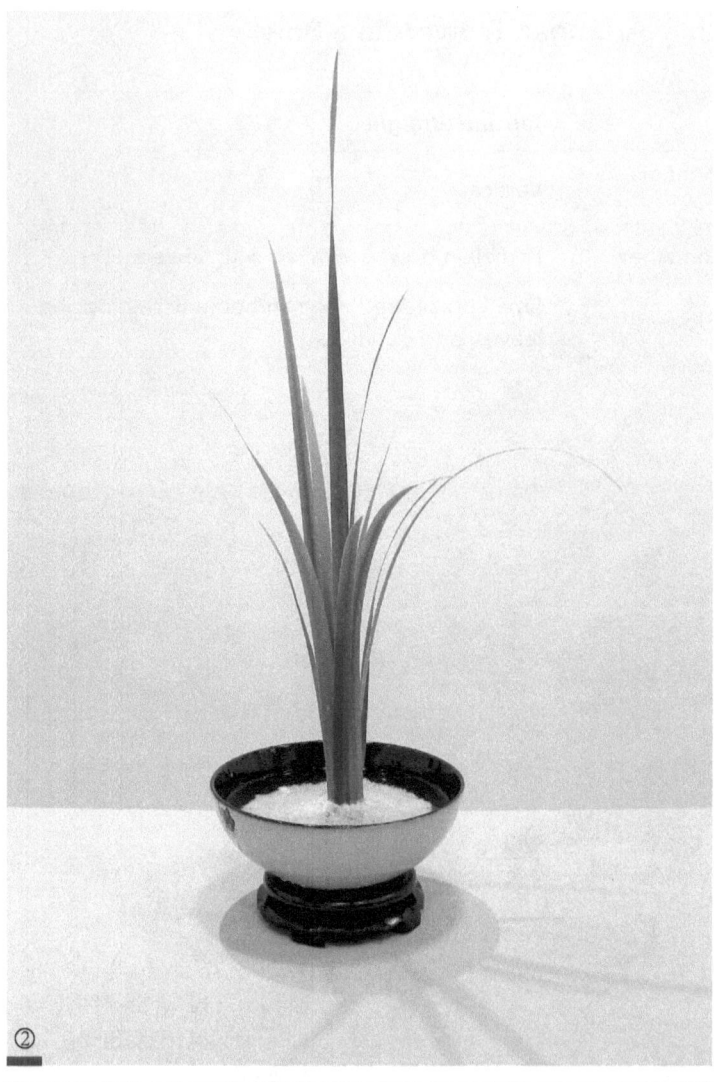

2. Choose iris leaves that are vertically upright, and pay close attention to the various layers. Next, select some curvy iris leaves to enhance the overall effect.

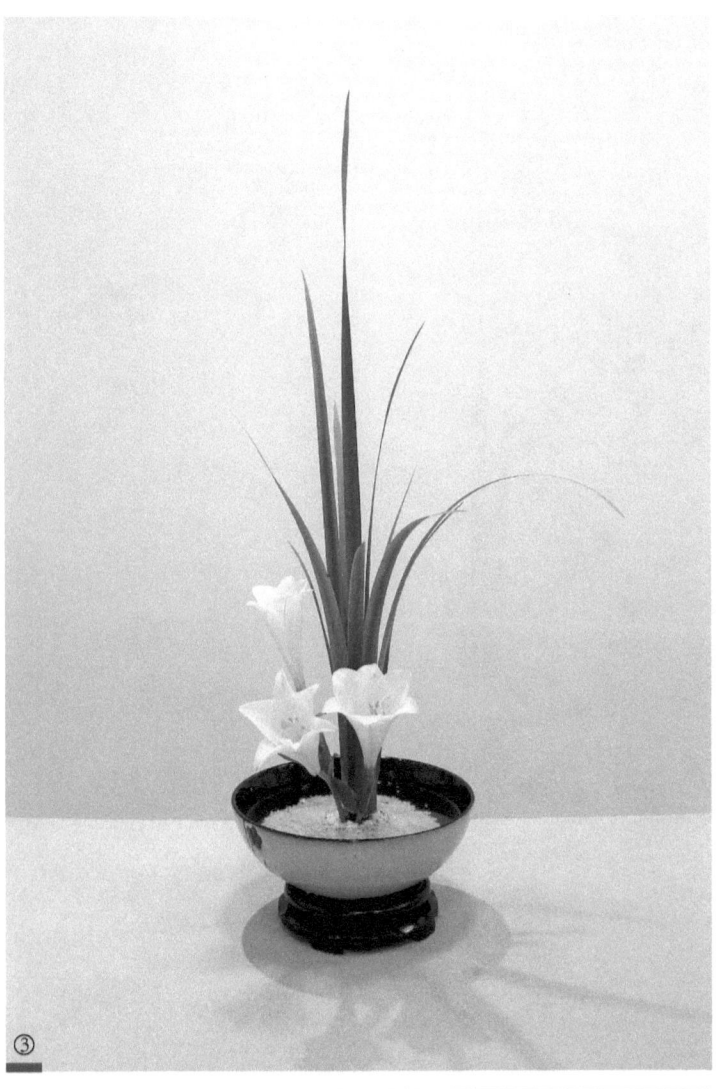

3. Add iron lilies at the lower portion, paying attention to the relationship between the space and layers of the flowers.

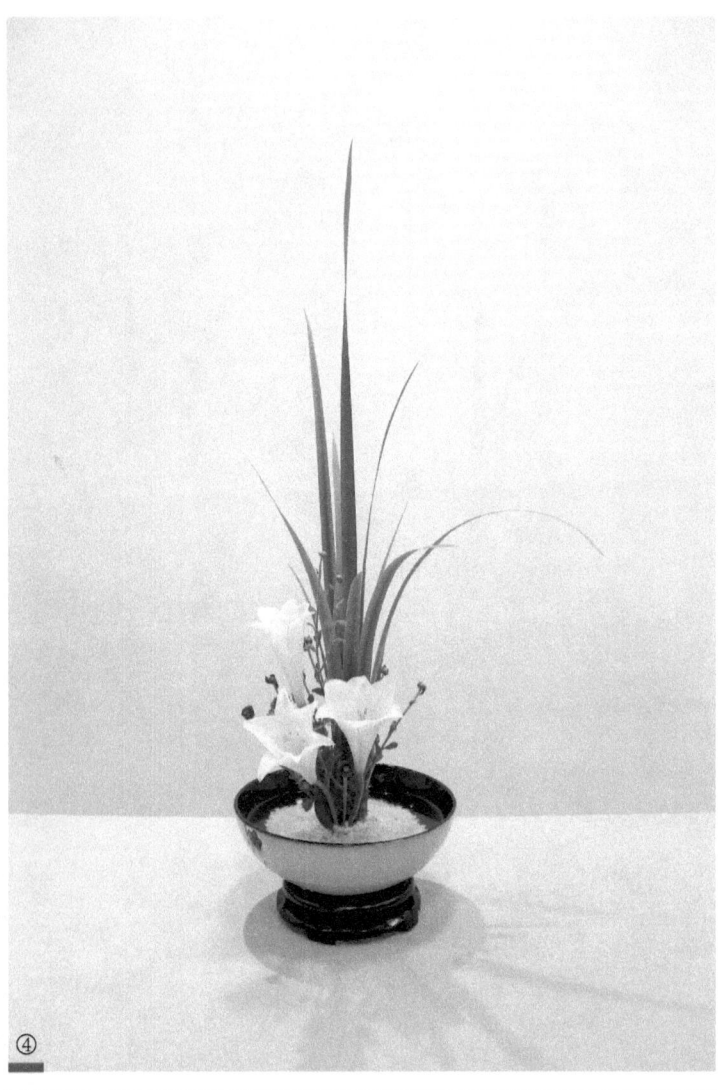

④

4. Add small purple-red chrysanthemums, focusing on layering with the main flowers.

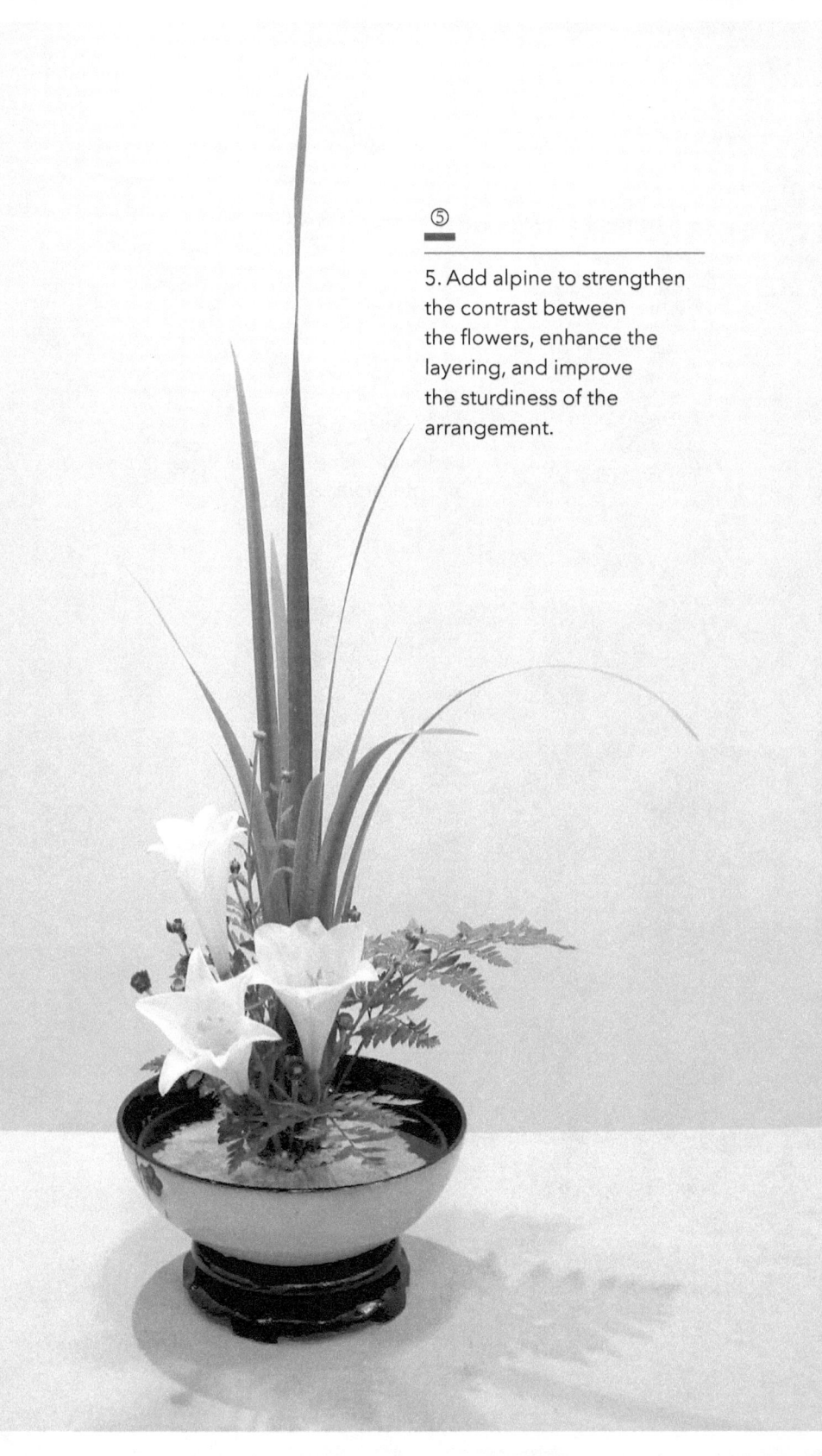

5. Add alpine to strengthen
the contrast between
the flowers, enhance the
layering, and improve
the sturdiness of the
arrangement.

3. Tilting Flowers on a Plate

Name	*Sunset*
Arrangement of Flowers	Tilting
Type of Container	Red porcelain pot
Types of Flowers	Red autumn leaves, sunflowers, Japanese privet, and *monstera*

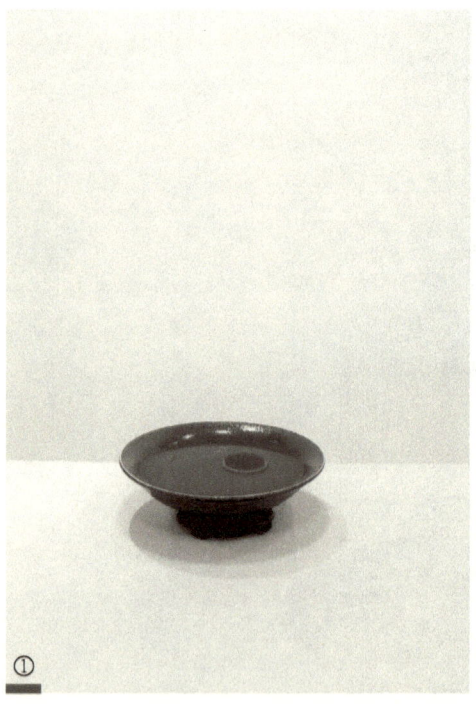

①

1. Select an aesthetically pleasing plate and place the *jianshan* device in the opposite direction of the tilting flowers.

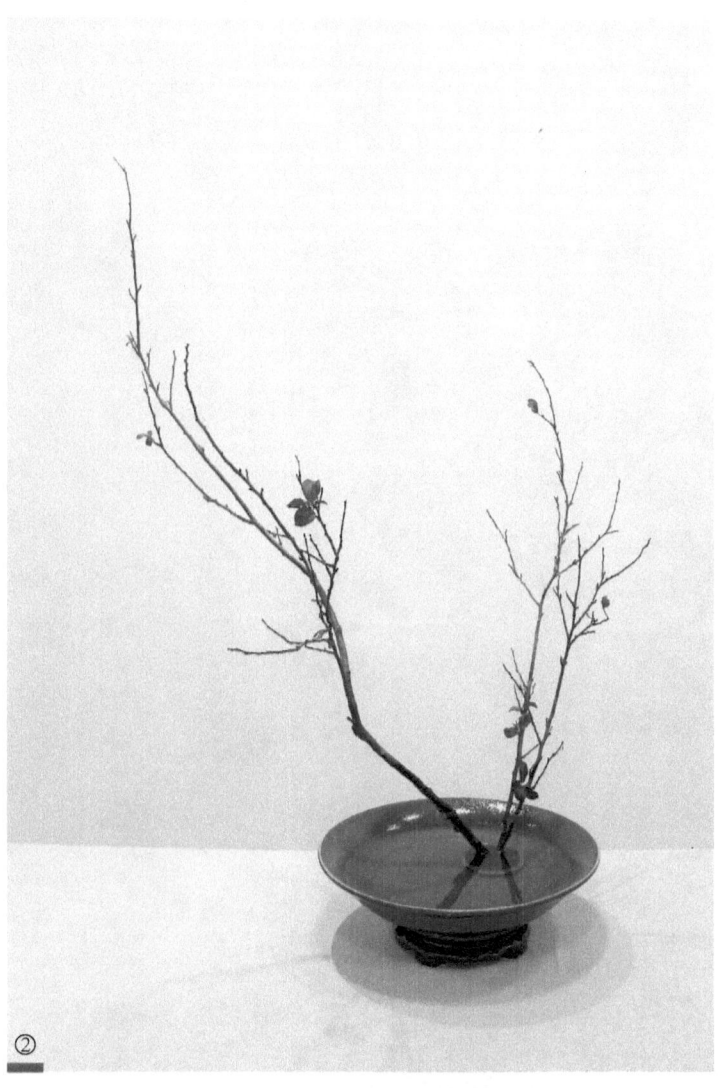

②

2. Select red autumnal leaves and tilting flower branches.
Insert them in the front and back of the frame, focusing on the
relationship between their heights and strengths.

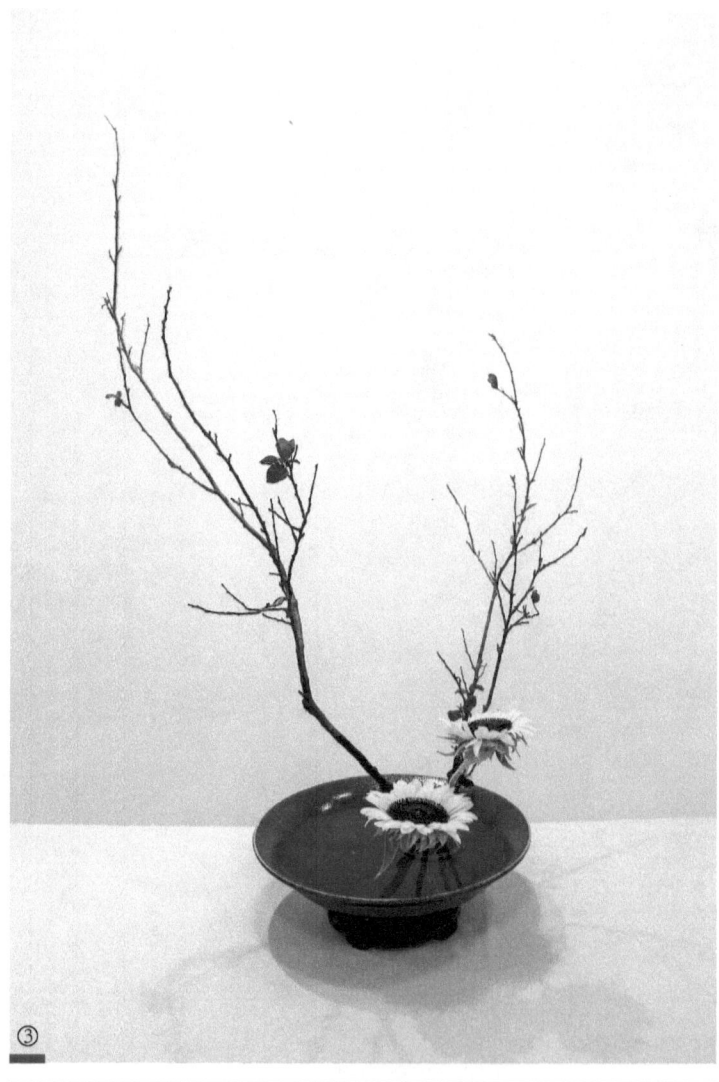

3. Add sunflowers to the base. Pay attention to the different heights and positions to highlight the main body and enhance the level of detail between each layer.

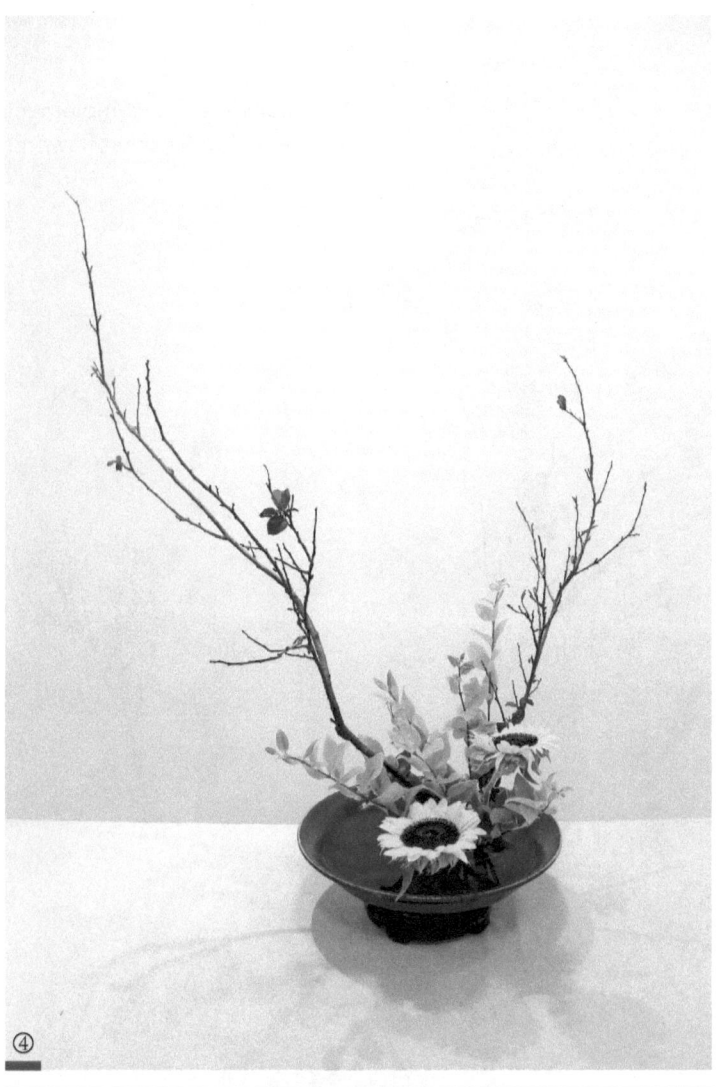

④

4. Add Japanese privet to complement the base and enhance the color contrast, while retaining the details and overall coherence.

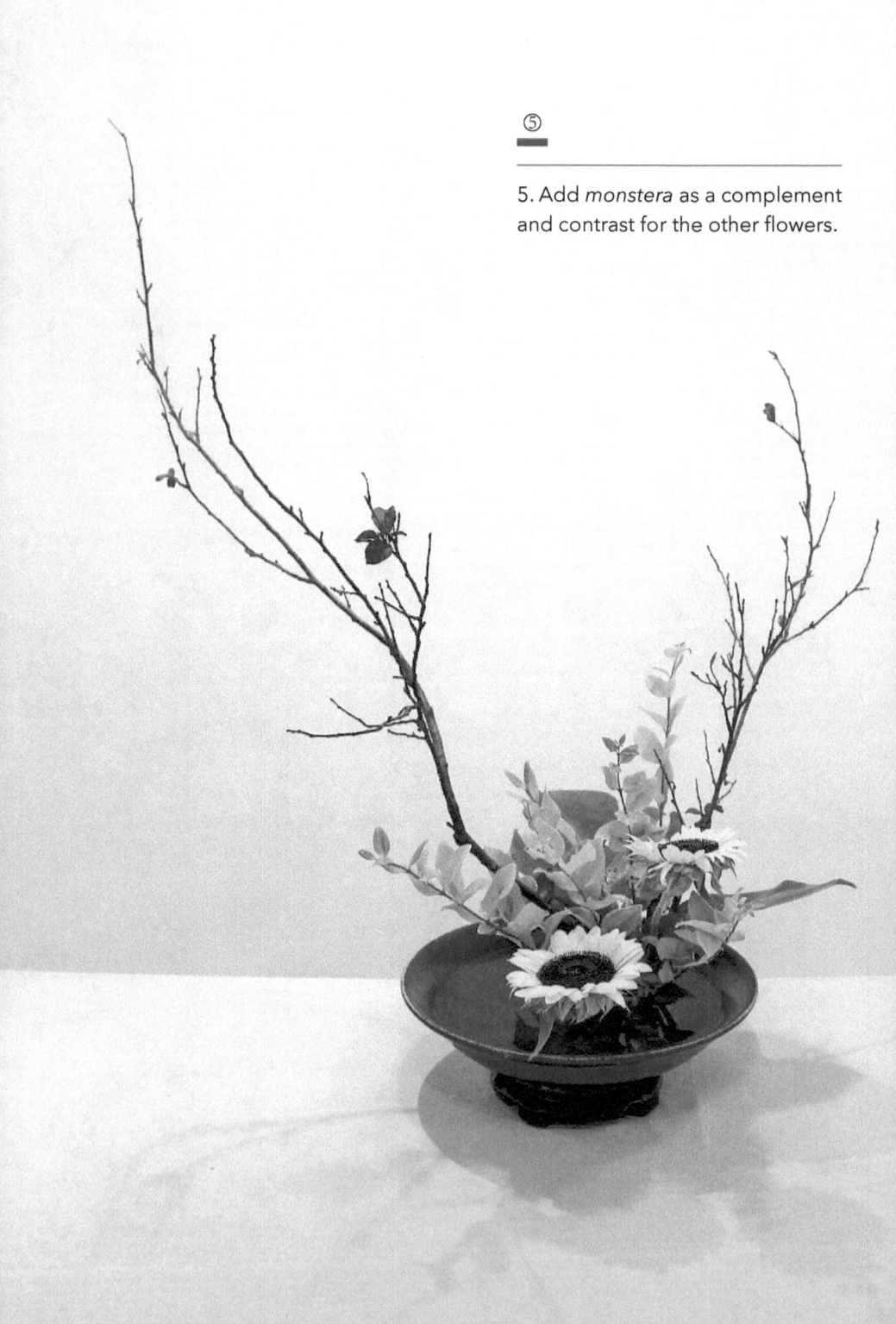

⑤

5. Add *monstera* as a complement and contrast for the other flowers.

4. Flowers Arranged in Flat Baskets

Name	*Titian*
Arrangement of Flowers	Flat
Type of Container	Bamboo basket
Types of Flowers	Red autumn leaves, pink roses, small white chrysanthemums, and *monstera*

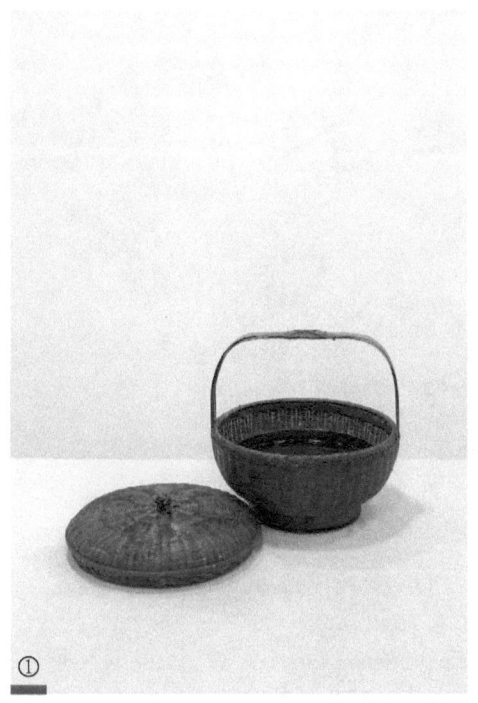

1. Choose an aesthetically appealing basket (preferably one that complements the colors of the plate) and fill it with water. Place the inner part of the plate and the tilting flowers in the opposite direction of the *jianshan*.

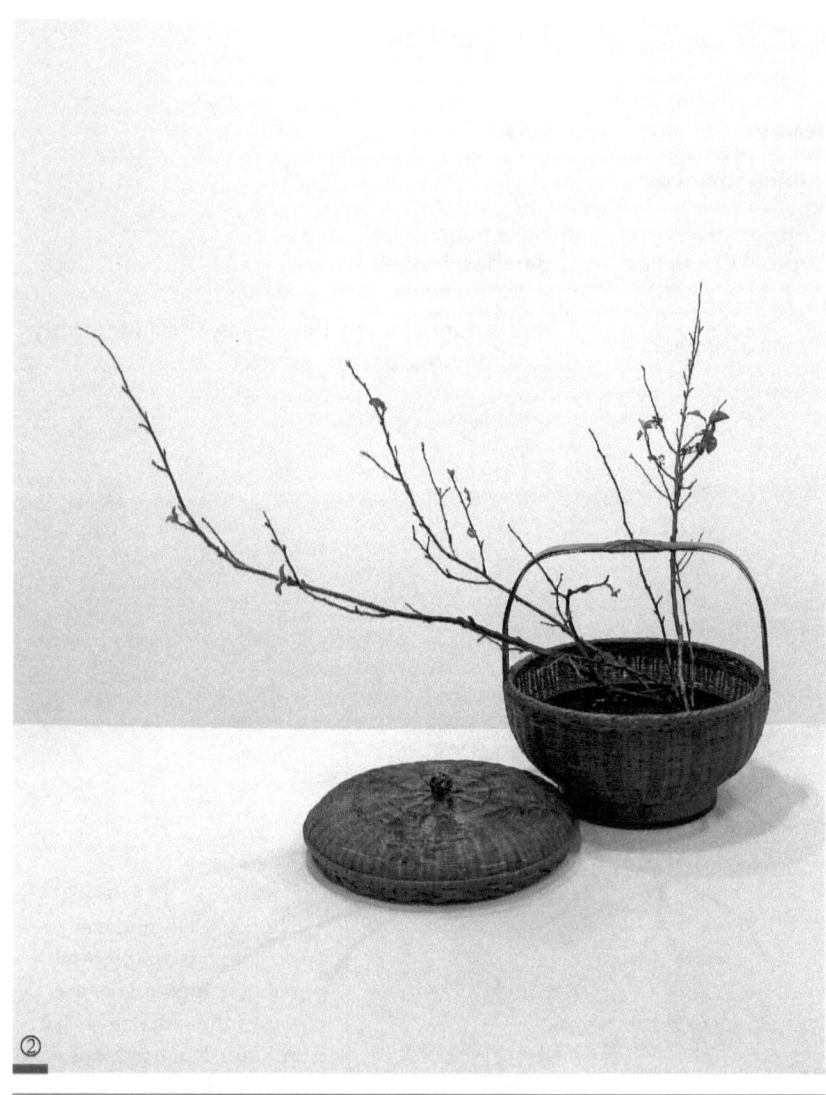

2. Select red autumnal leaves with flat branches, focusing on positioning of the flowers. To reflect their vitality, the branches should not lean against the flower basket.

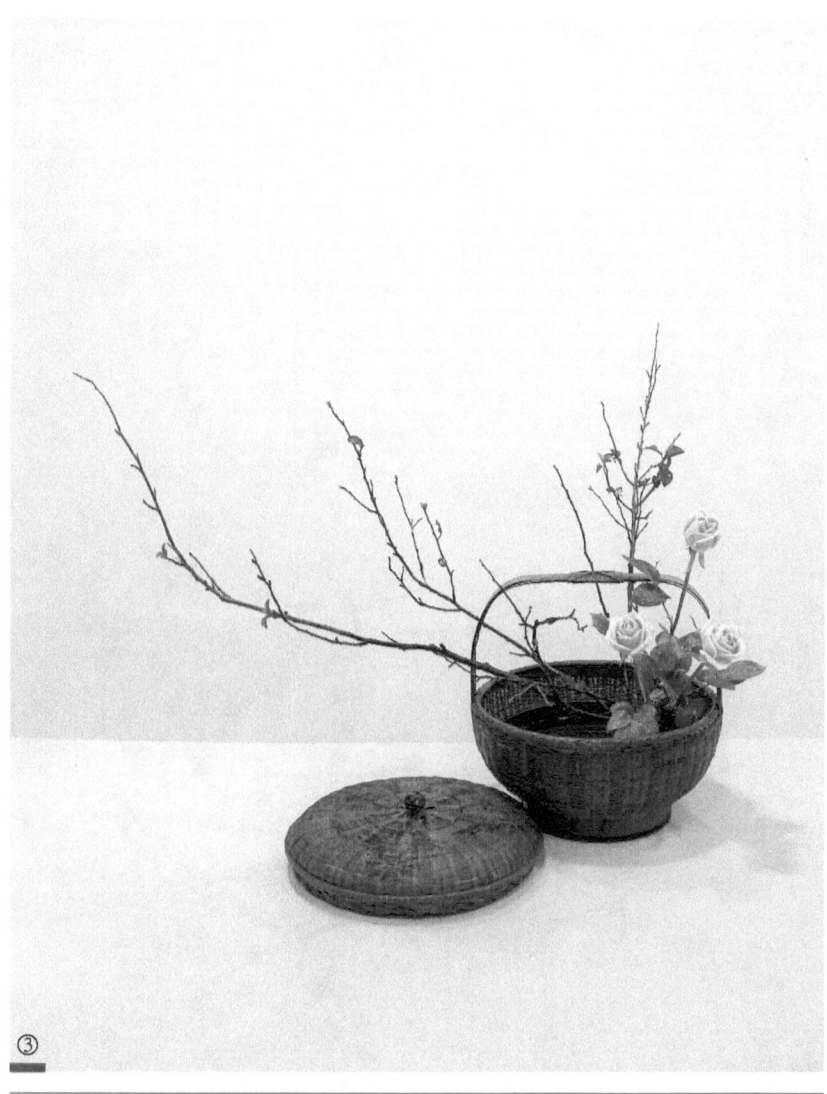

③

3. Add upright pink roses as the focal flowers, focusing on spacing, position, and denseness. The roses should not lean against the branches, basket handle, or basket body.

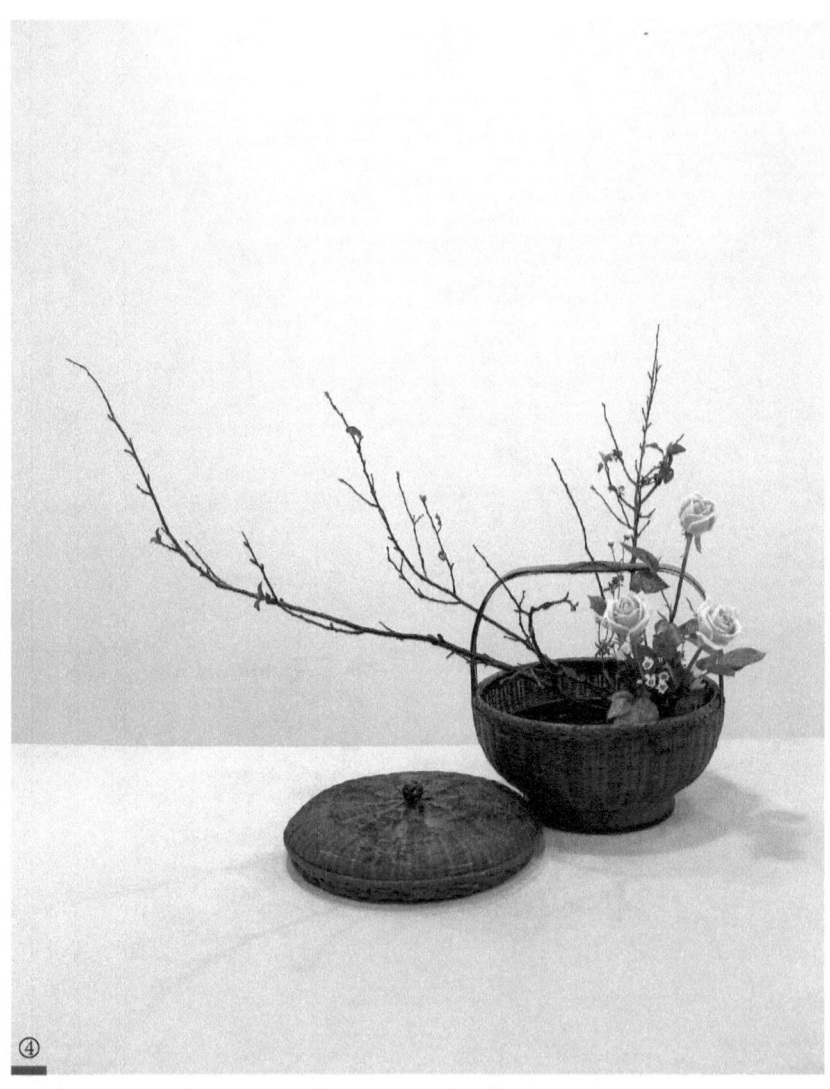

4. Add small white chrysanthemum flowers and buds to complement and enhance the base. Pay attention to both the main flowers and the supplementary blooms, particularly their height, spacing, and position.

5. Add monstera to complement and enhance the arrangement while adding contrast to the spacing flowers.

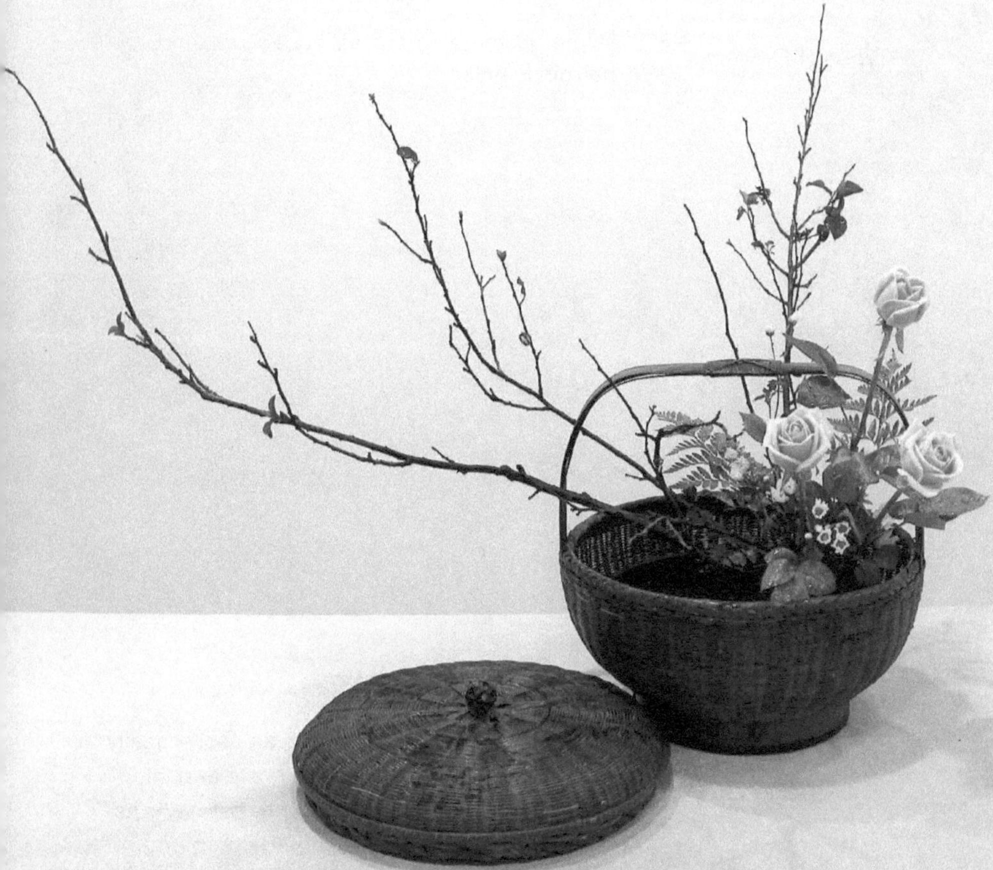

5. Hanging Flowers Arranged in a Vase

Name	*Yearning*
Arrangement of Flowers	Hanging
Type of Container	Blue-glazed okho spring bottles
Types of Flowers	Winter jasmine, red roses, *hypericum*, and hairpin leaves

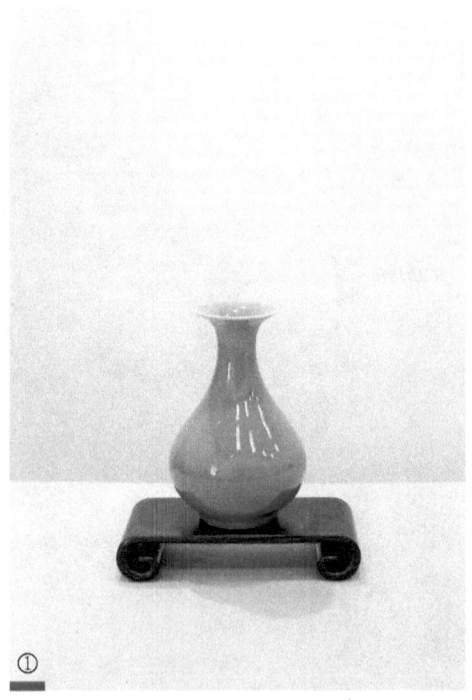

1. Choose an aesthetically appealing vase and fill it with water to the neck. Its style should complement the type of flowers used.

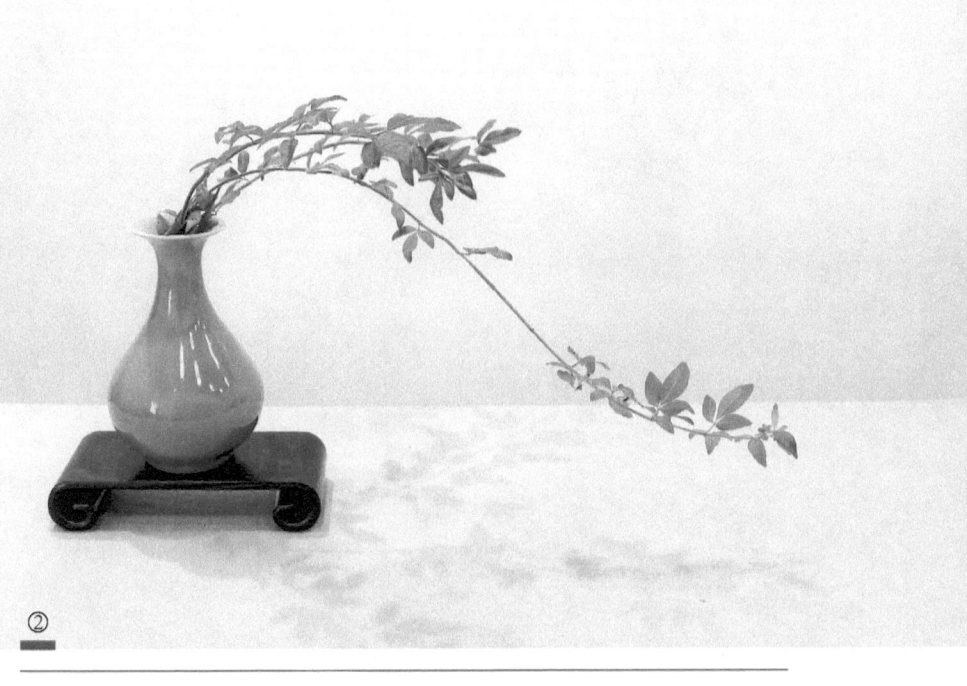

②

2. Select the focal flowers (white jasmine branches) and place them into the vase to form a contrast with the complementary flowers. Pay attention to the branches, particularly their space, length, and layers.

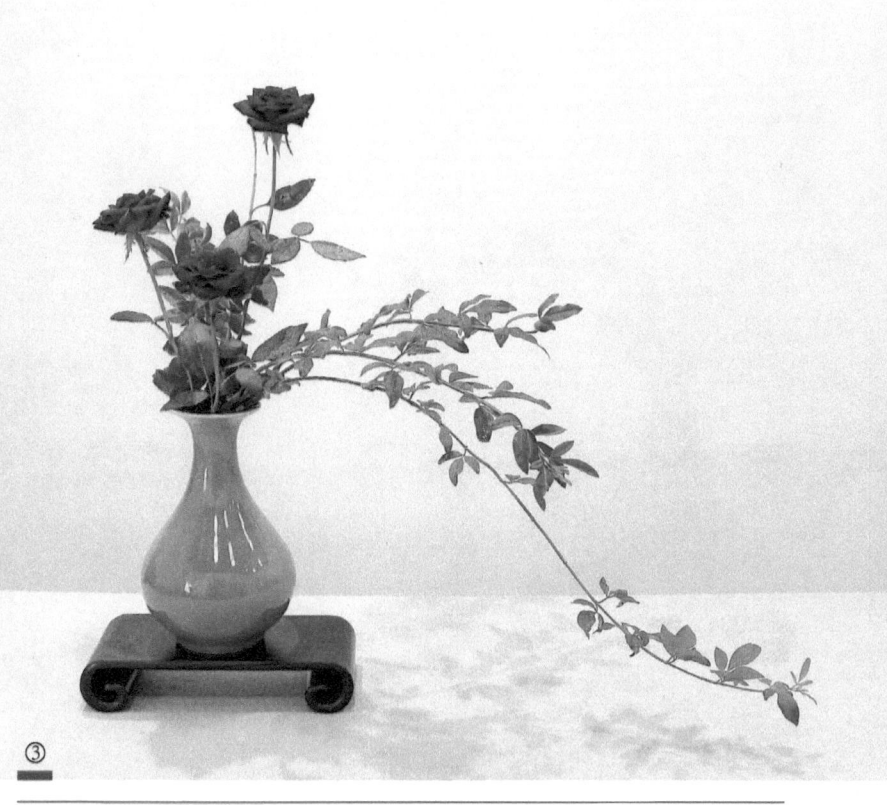

③

3. Add pink roses as the main body of the arrangement. Scatter them around the main flowers, paying attention to differences in their height, layers, and space. Add the back portion of the white jasmine branches for support.

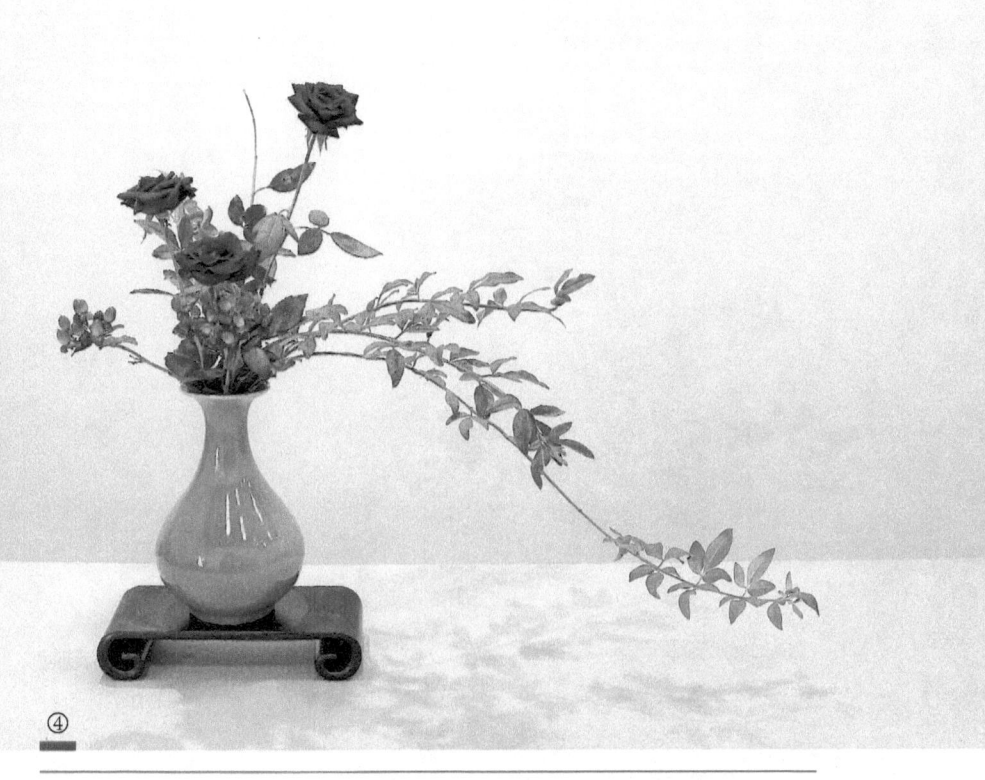

④

4. Add *hypericum*. The colors and main body should be synchronized to bring out subtle changes. Pay attention to enhancing the relationship between the main and complementary flowers, particularly the changes in height and space.

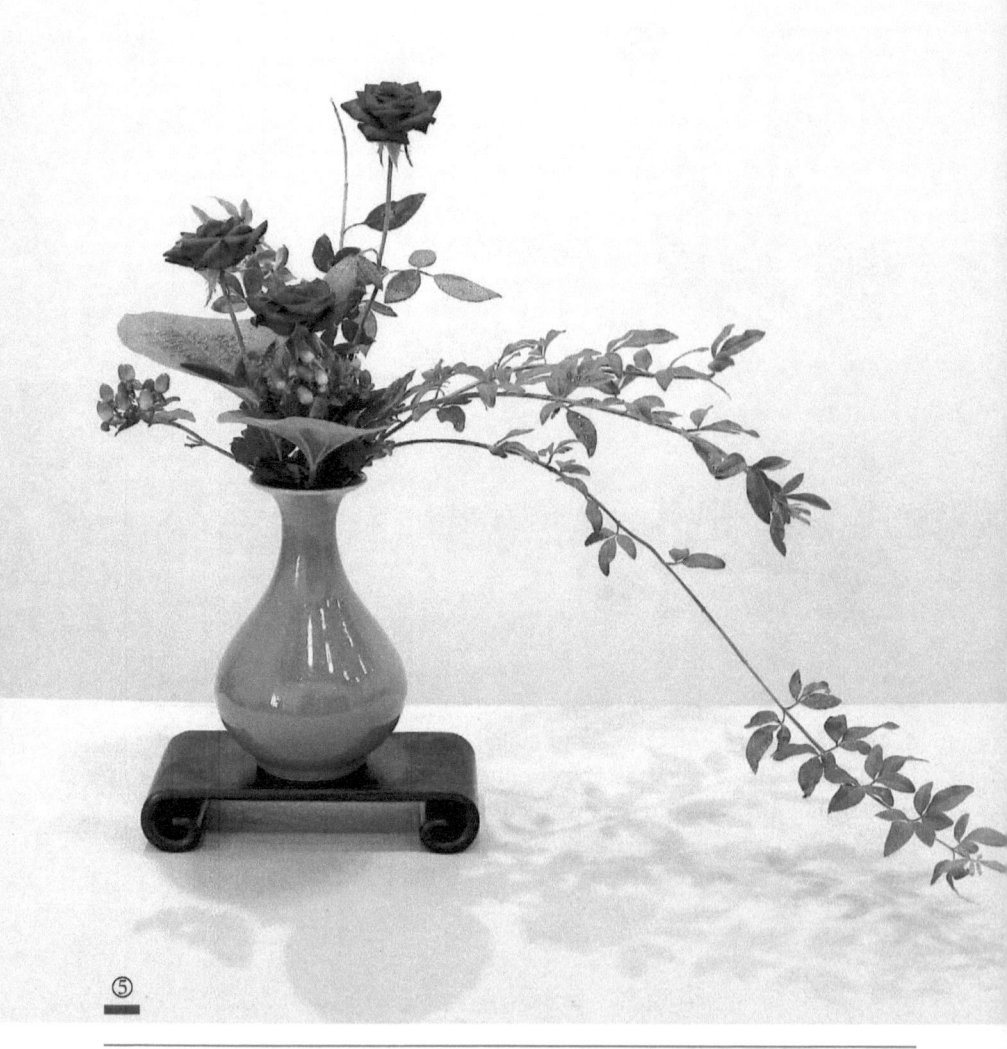

5. Scatter hairpin leaves to bring about a contrast between the types of flowers, enabling the focal blooms to stand out.

6. Flowers Arranged in a Flat Dish

Name	*Flying*
Arrangement of Flowers	Flat
Type of Container	Black porcelain dish
Types of Flowers	*Pleione formosana, lisianthus, photinia fraseri,* and *fatsia japonica*

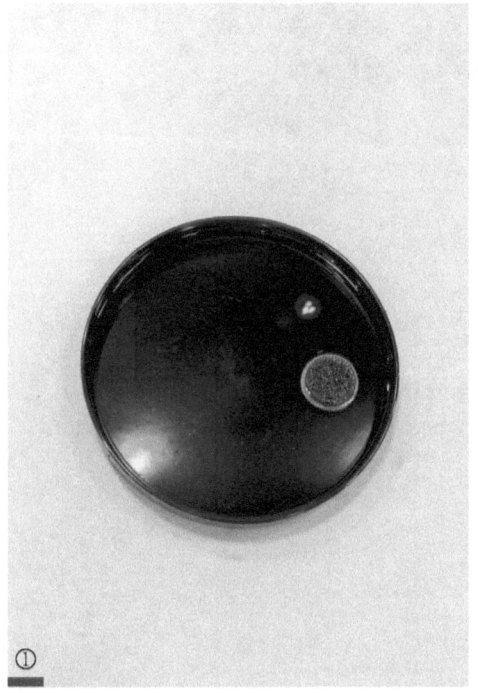

1. Select an aesthetically pleasing dish that complements the work, with a *jianshan* at the side. The work should be viewed from above.

45

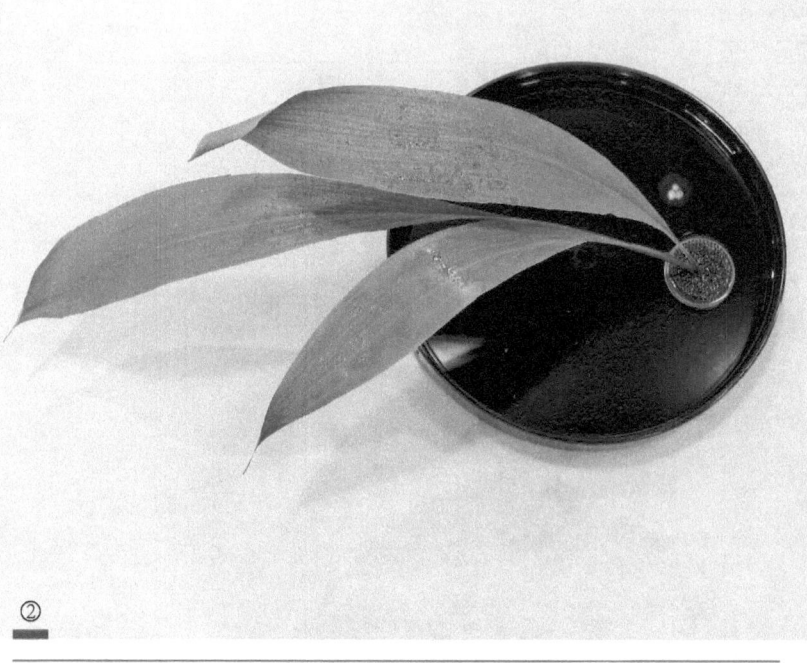

②

2. Add *pleione formosana* branches to support the second frame. Pay attention to the overall spacing, while highlighting the overall direction of momentum.

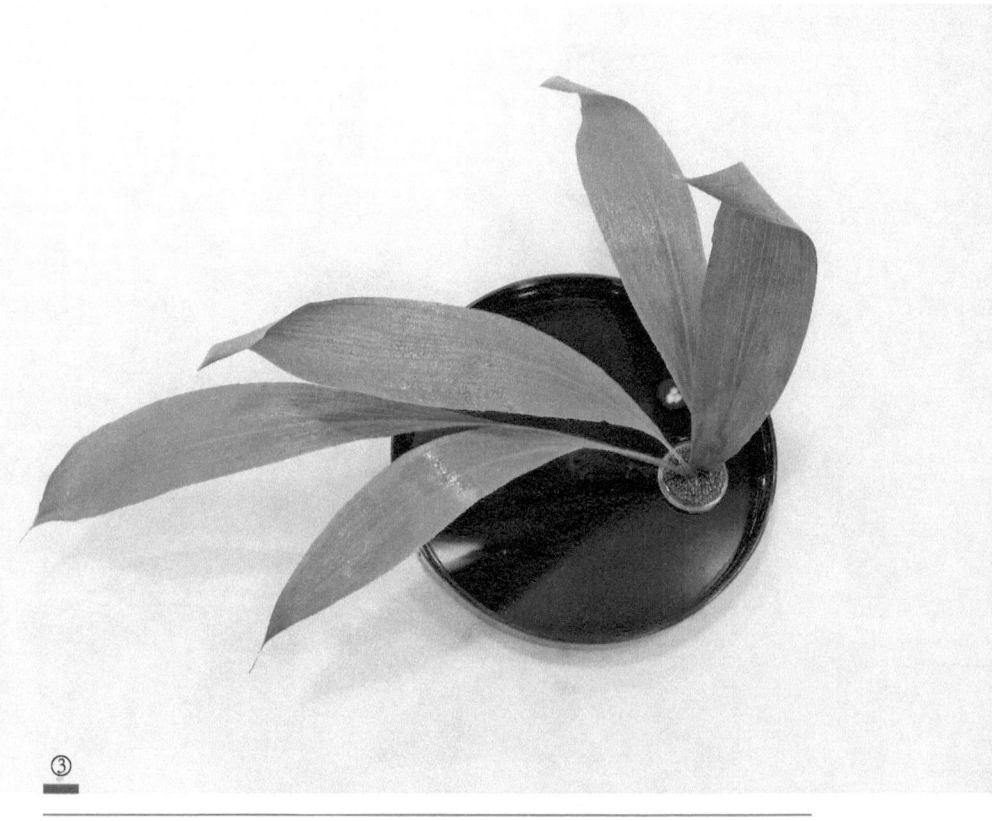

③

3. Add *pleione formosana* – the main flowers for the frame. When inserting them into the frame, pay attention to the spaces between the leaves and bundles to emphasize the vitality of the arrangement.

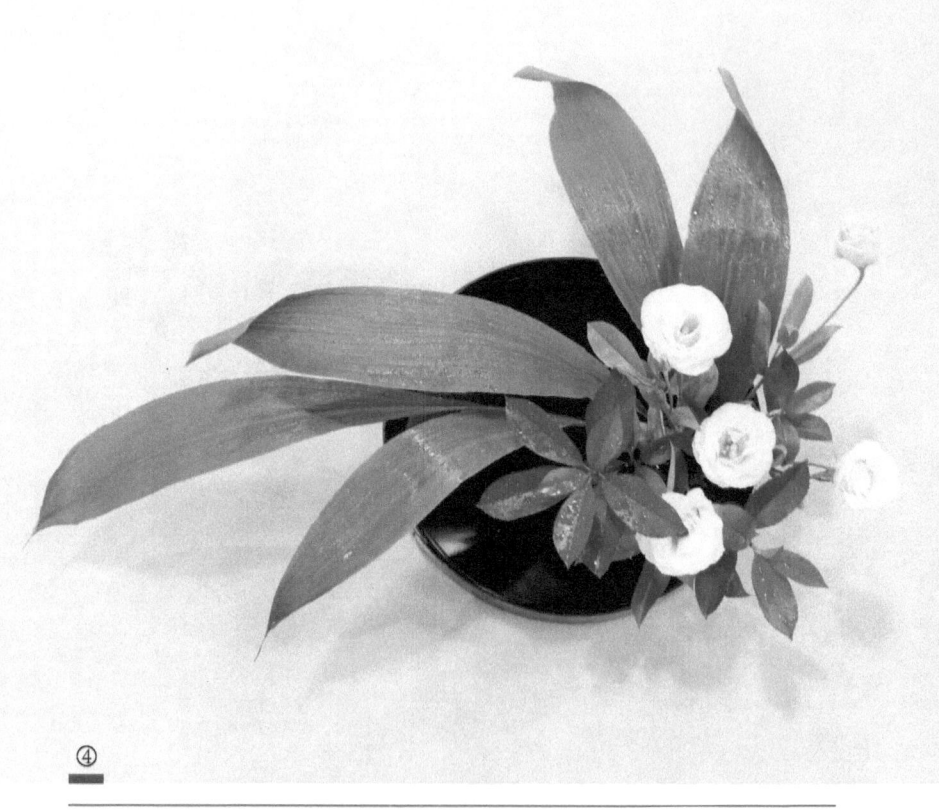

④

4. Add the focal blooms (*lisianthus*) with both the flowers and buds, scattering them around the main body. Add the complementary *photinia fraseri* to form a contrast that enhances the overall effect.

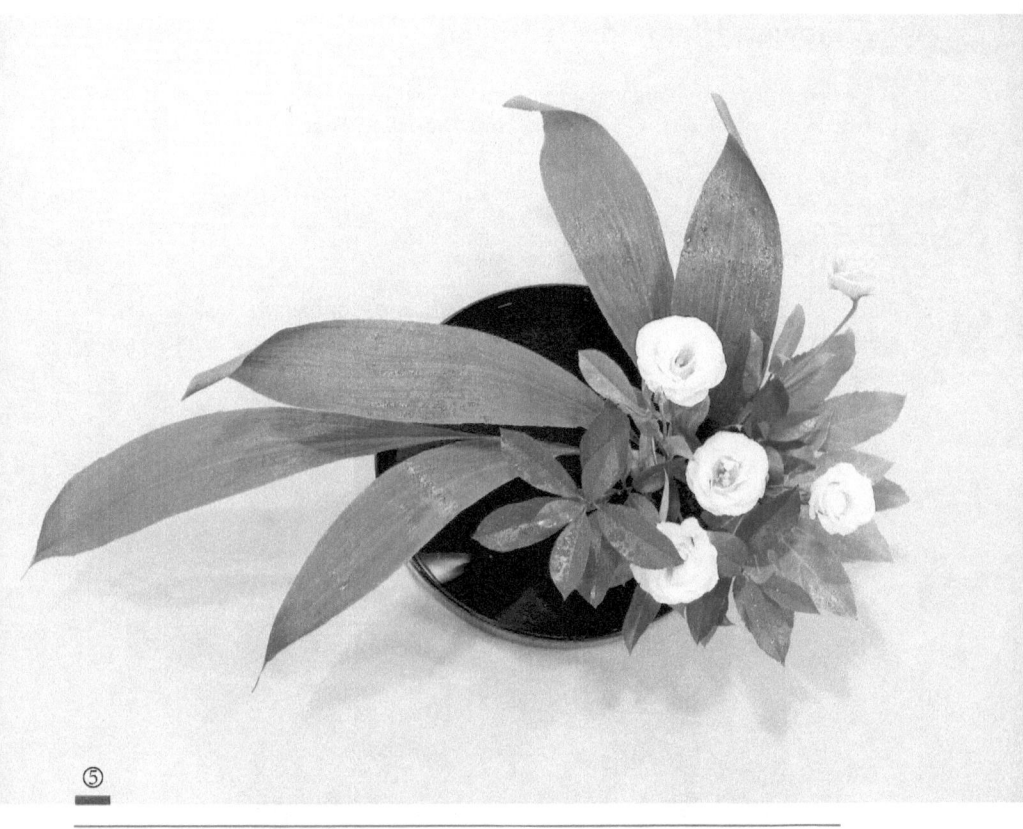

⑤

5. Scatter hairpin leaves to bring about a contrast between the types of flowers, enabling the focal blooms to stand out.

7. Flowers Hung Upside Down

Name	*Flying Three Thousand Feet*
Arrangement of Flowers	Upside down
Type of Container	Bamboo tube
Types of Flowers	*Chenopodium formosanum koidz*, golden lily, white flowers, small chrysanthemum, and *aspidistra elatior*

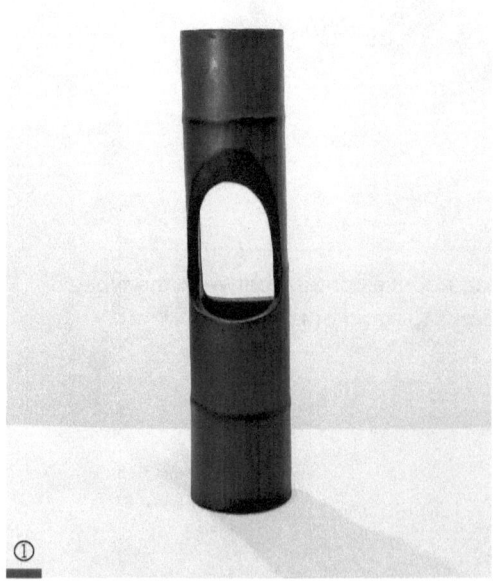

1. Select an aesthetically pleasing bamboo tube and fill it with gravel. Add a *jianshan* of an appropriate size.

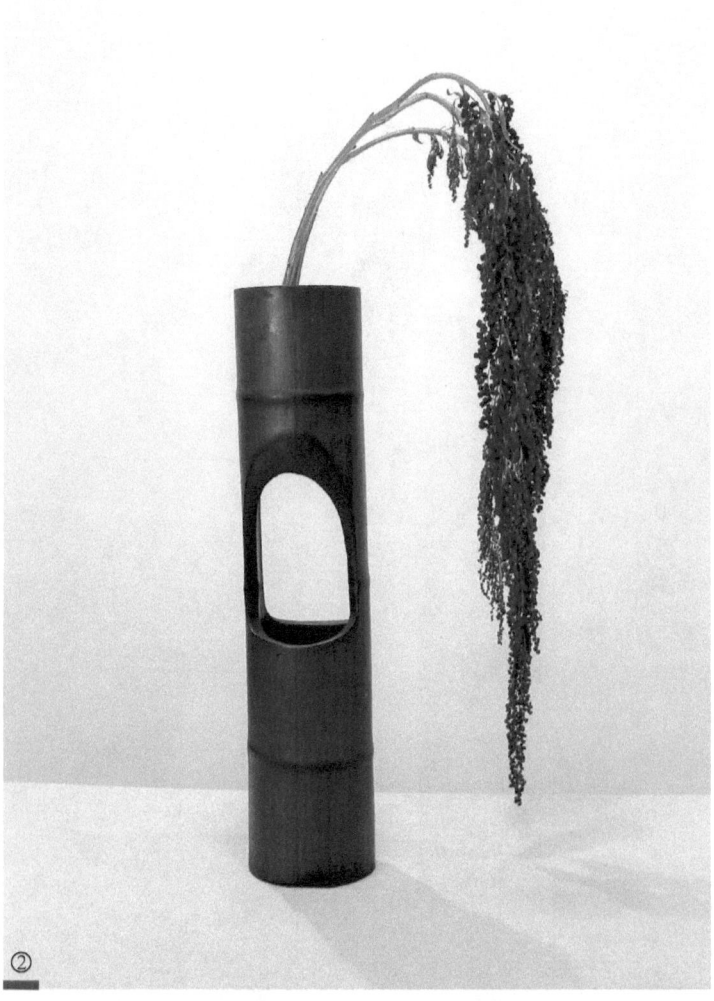

②

2. Hang the main flowers (*chenopodium formosanum koidz*) upside down, ensuring that there is adequate distance between it and the ground. The branches should not lean against the wall or other parts of the tube, and should be inserted as a bundle.

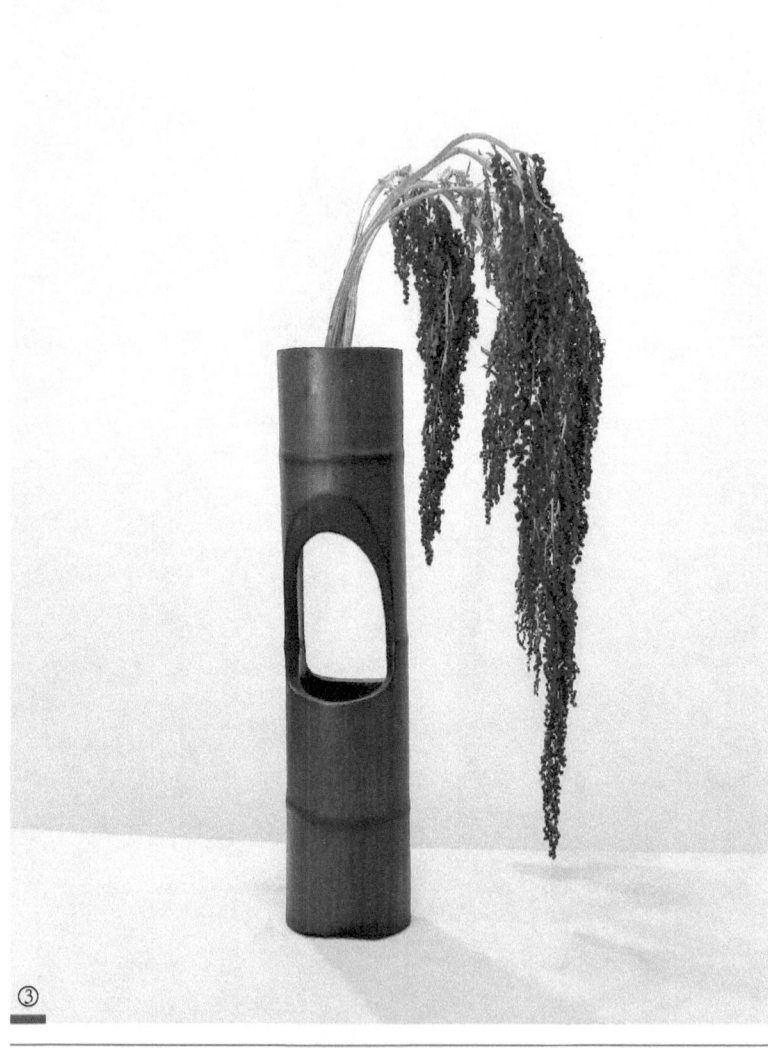

③

3. Add *chenopodium formosanum koidz* to the second frame, and place other flowers behind it. It should be able to support the arrangement when placed upright, with a clear distinction between the main and secondary bodies, as well as plenty of space.

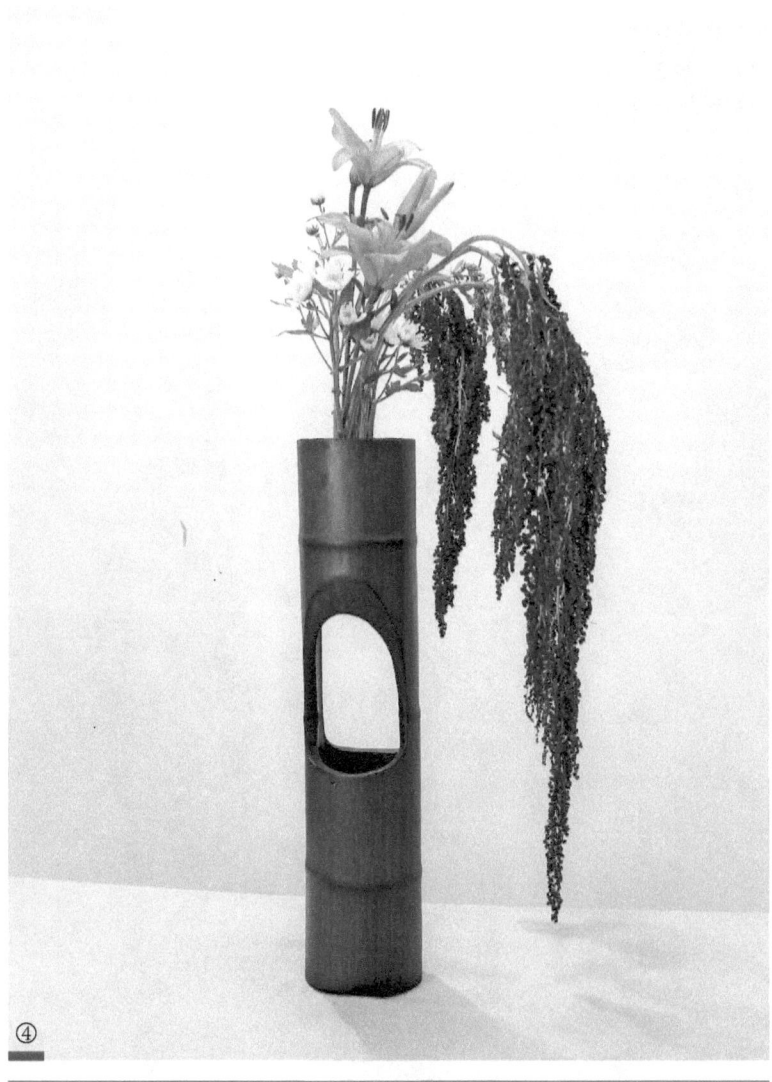

④

4. Add the main blooms (golden lilies), with the flowers and buds intact. Pay attention to the height and scattered branches. Add white flowers and small chrysanthemums to complement the base and main body.

5. Add *aspidistra elatior* to bring out
the contrast among the other flowers.
Pay attention to changes in space,
length, and height.

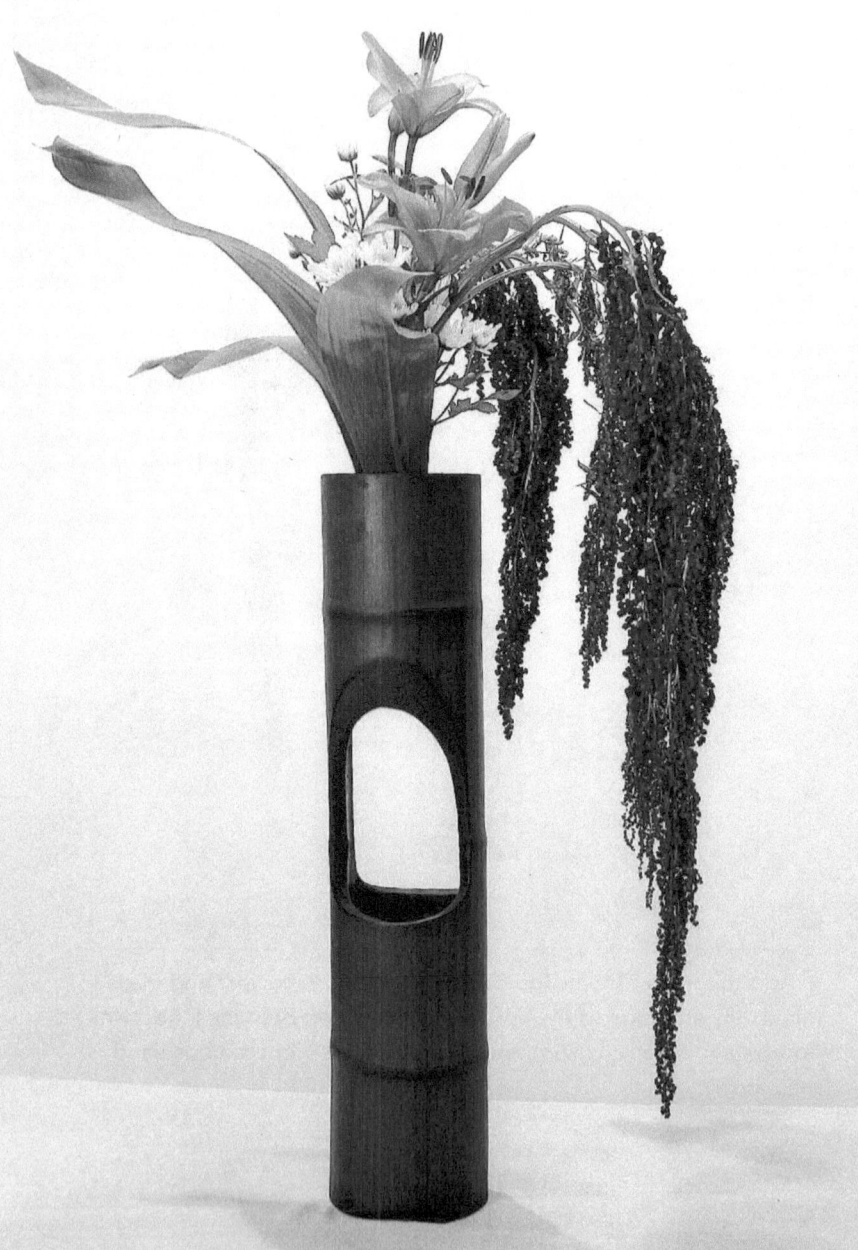

8. Integrated Vessels

Name	*Washing in the Creek*
Arrangement of Flowers	Flat
Type of Container	Black porcelain/plastic dish
Types of Flowers	*Ilex cornuta var. fortunei*, hibiscus, *celosia argentea, and allium funckiaefolium*

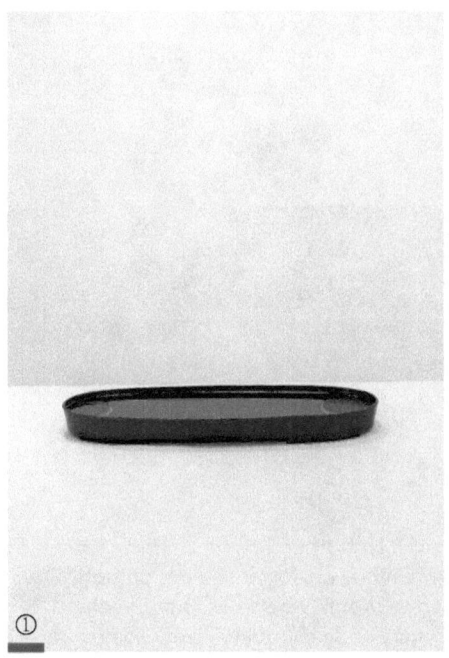

1. Select a long, aesthetically appealing basin that is compatible with floral patterns. Place a jianshan on both the left and right sides of it.

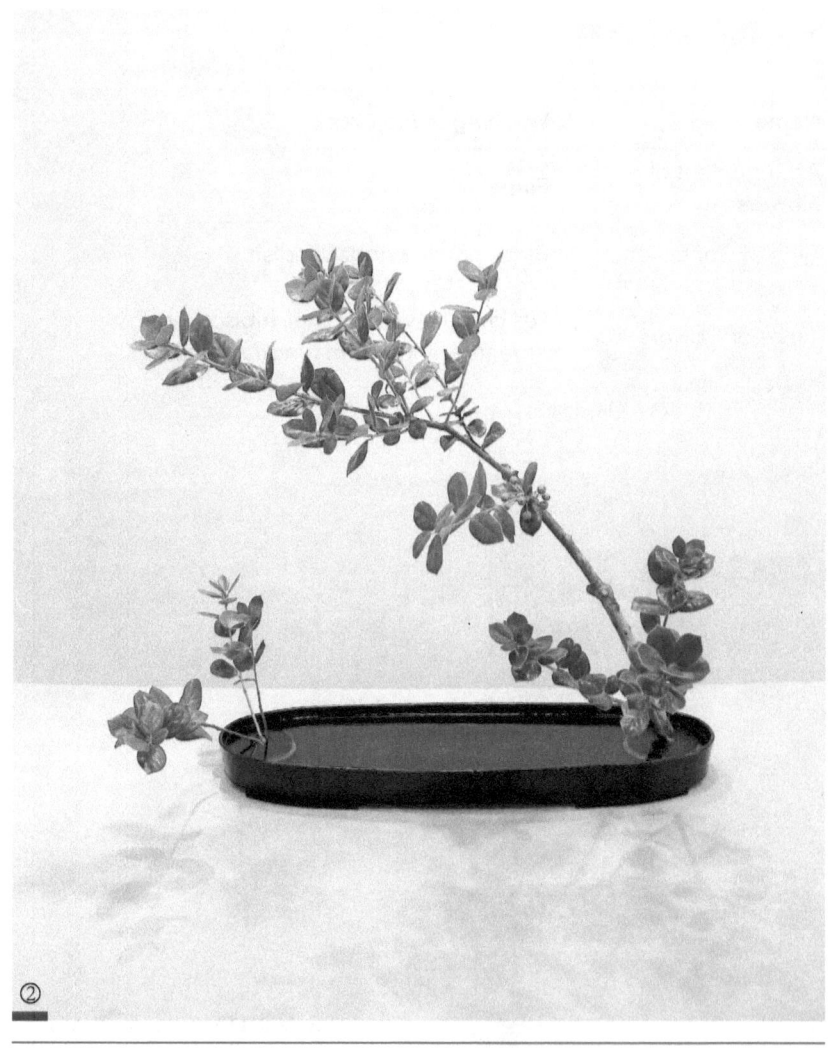

2. Insert *ilex cornuta var. fortunei* (the main flowers for the frame) on both sides of the frame concurrently. Pay attention to mobility between the branches, and to the distinction between the primary and secondary layers, to ensure coherence.

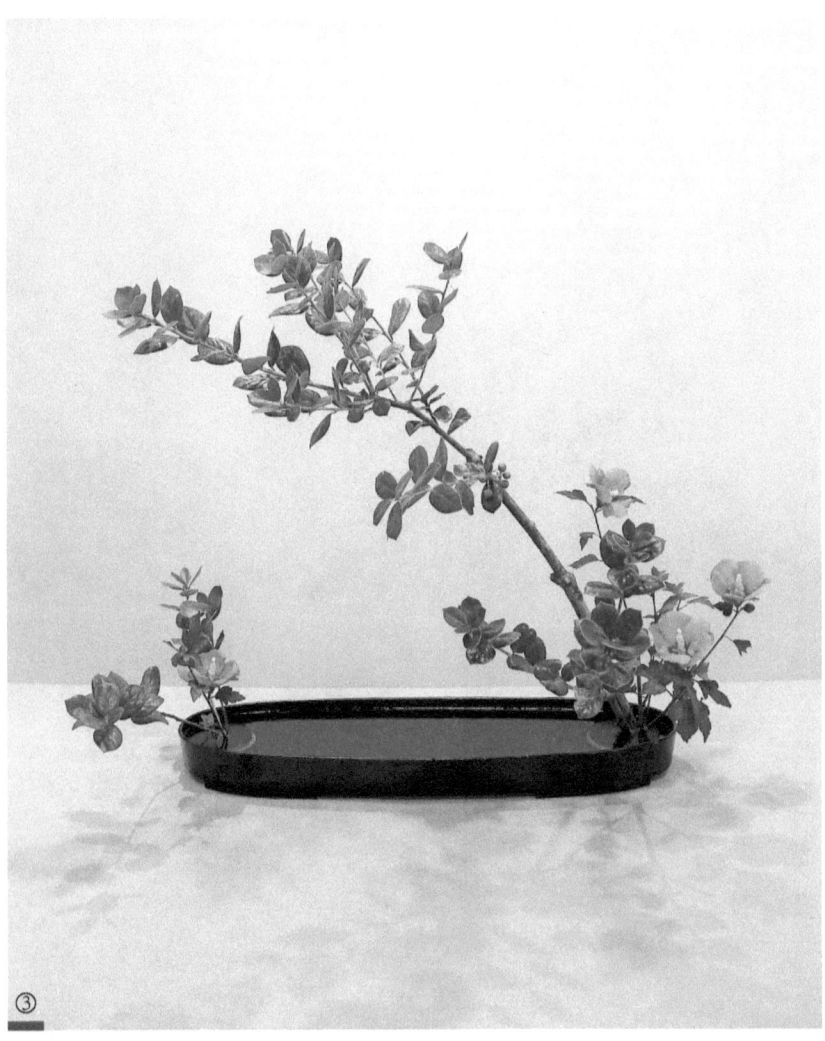

3. Scatter the main flowers (hibiscus) around the main body, creating harmony between the primary and secondary bodies to accentuate their beauty.

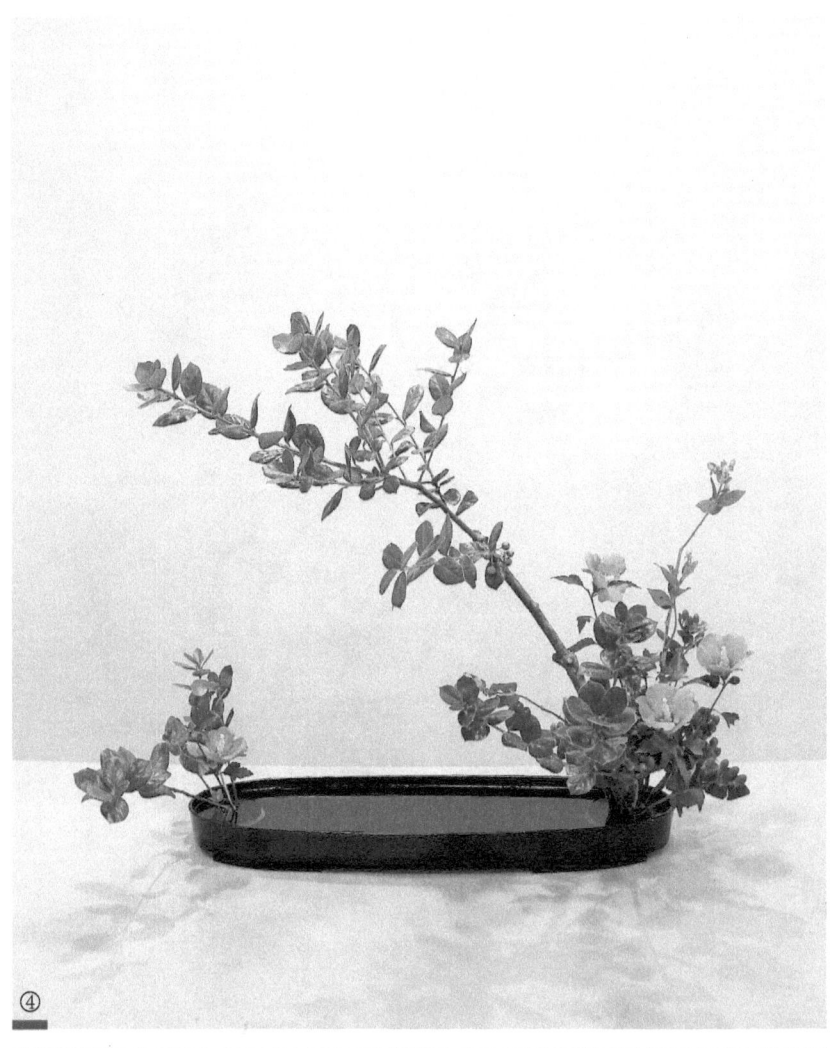

④

4. Add *hypericum* to complement the base and form different levels of denseness and height between the flowers.

5. Add *allium funckiaefolium* to
complement the base and form a
contrast with the other flowers. Pay
attention to the use of proportion
and space between leaves.

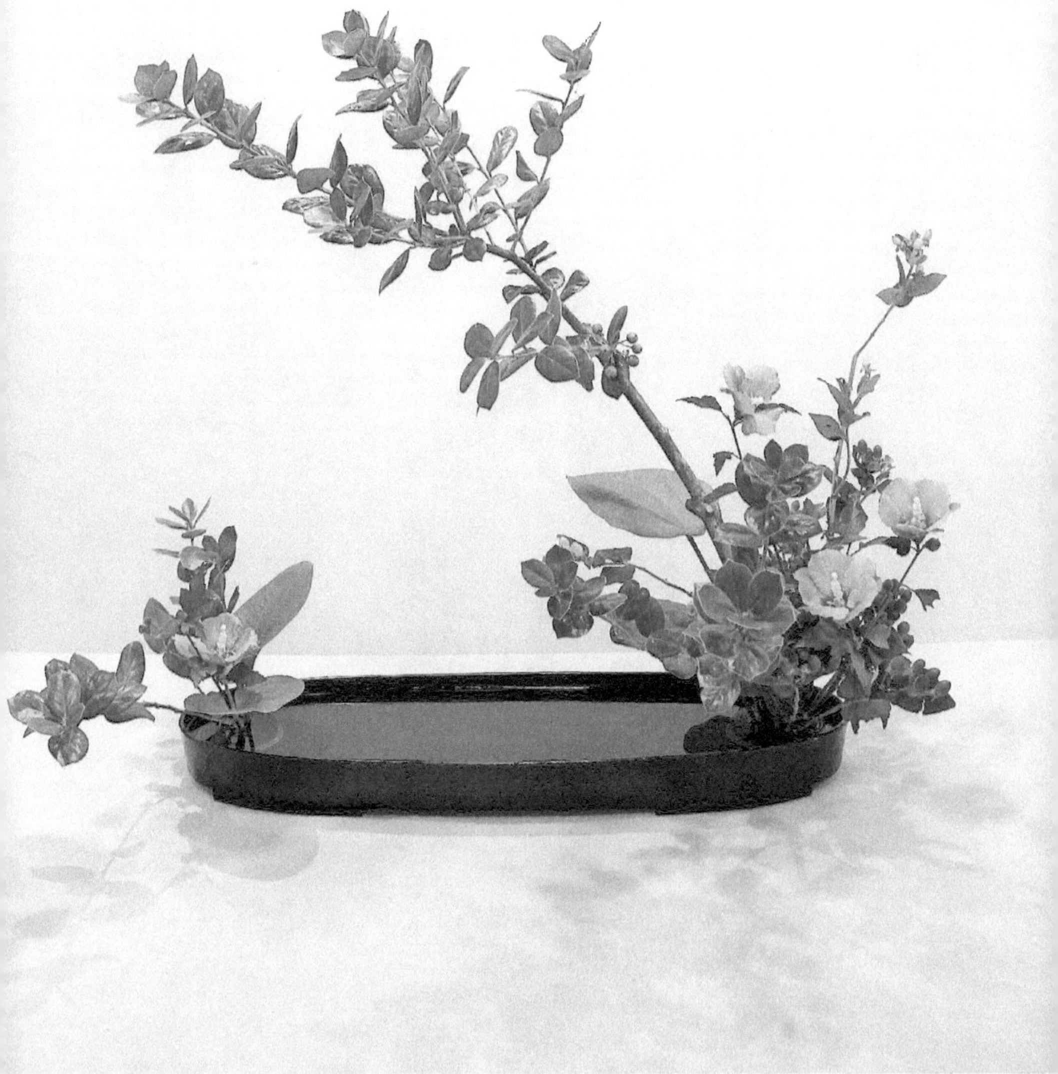

4

ANALYSIS
OF CHINESE FLOWER
ARRANGEMENTS

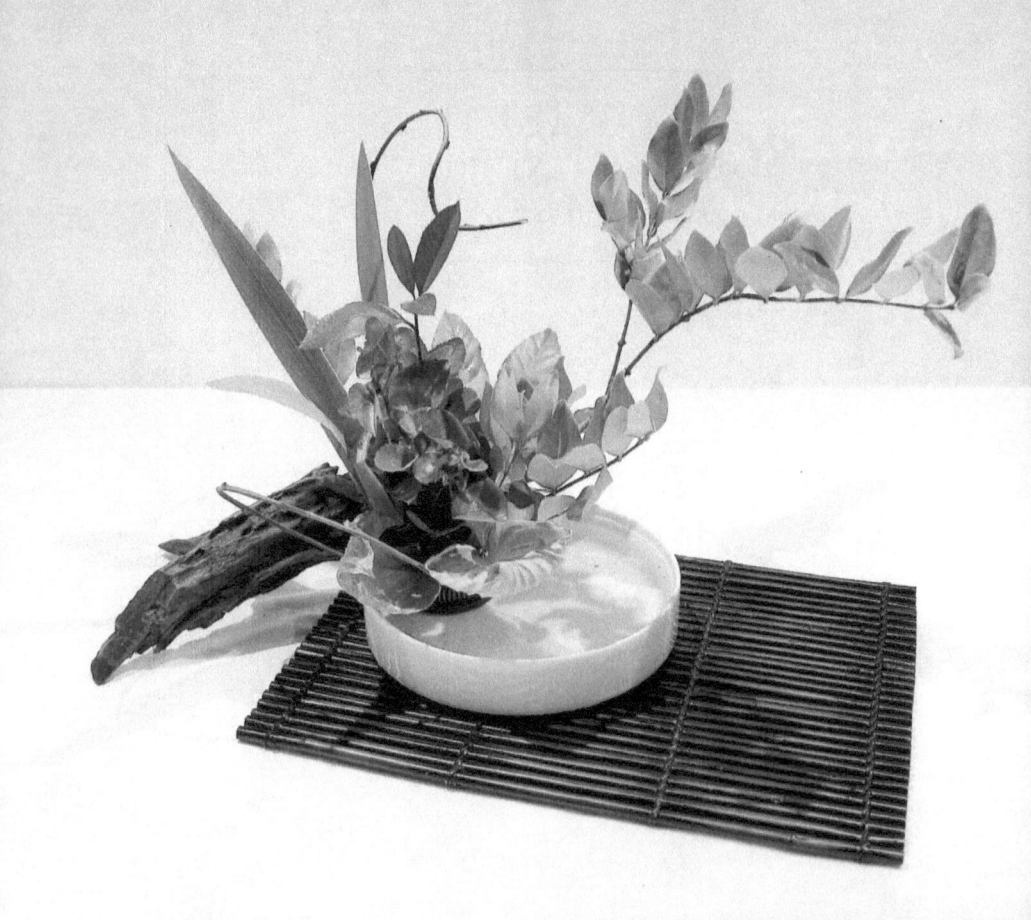

Blooming Flowers in Shallow Water

Type of Arrangement	Tilting
Type of Container	White ceramic plate
Types of Flowers	*Ligustrum japonicum 'Howardii', photinia fraseri,* iris leaf, wax begonia, hairpin leaves, and star anise

Silent Rogue

Type of Arrangement	Tilting
Type of Container	Green ceramic bowl
Types of Flowers	*Loropetalum chinense var. rubrum,* wax begonia, and *silver ragwort*

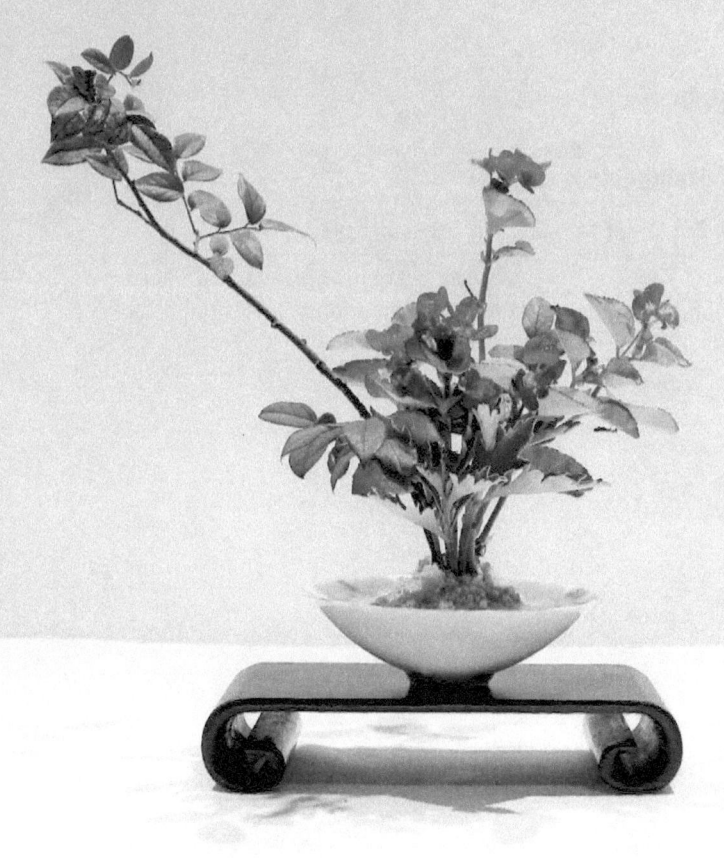

Floating on Red Water

Type of Arrangement	Tilting
Type of Container	Round ceramic plate
Types of Flowers	Wisteria branch, *liriope muscari 'variegata'*, *curcuma alsimatifolia,* and small white chrysanthemum

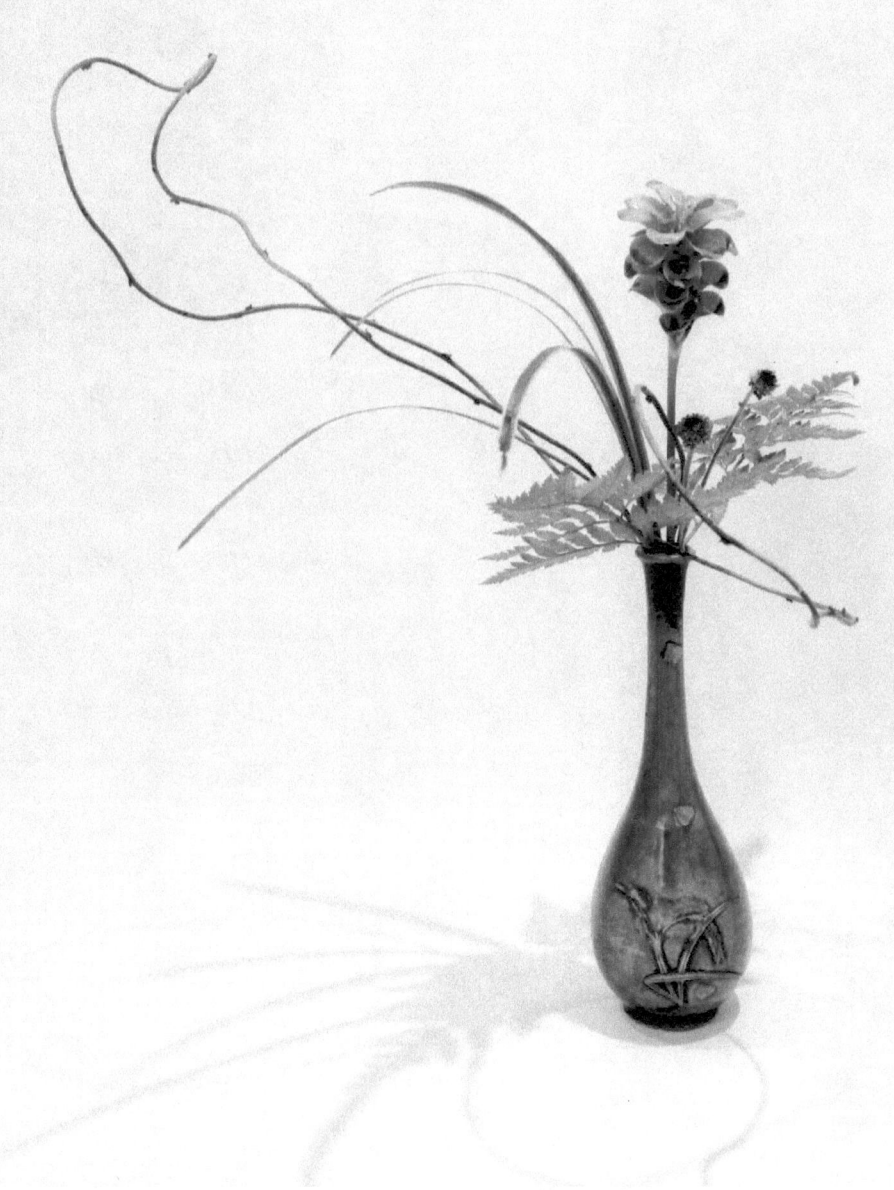

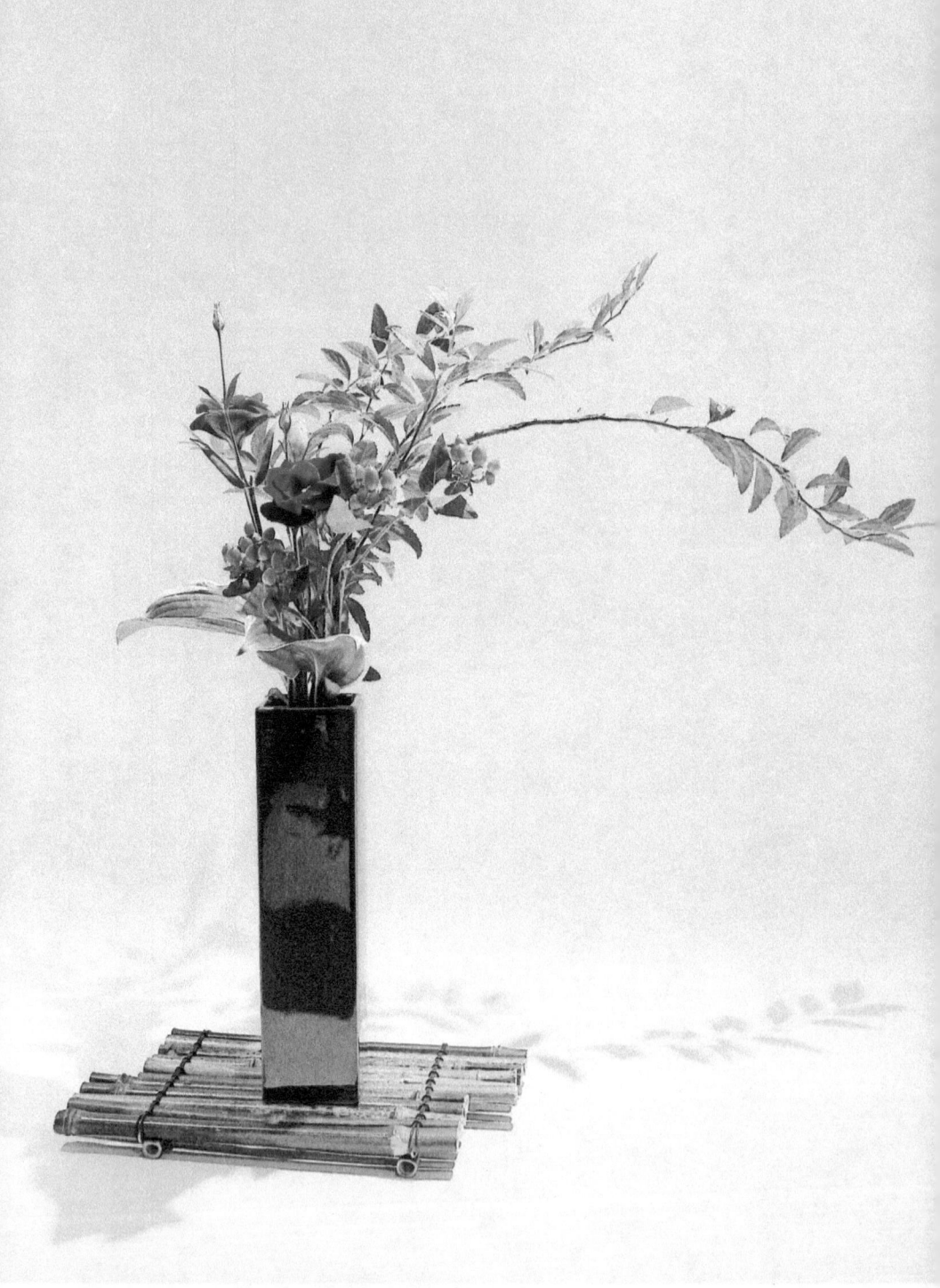

Beautiful Amethyst

Type of Arrangement	Flat
Type of Container	Square porcelain vase
Types of Flowers	Winter jasmine, *lisianthus*, *celosia argentea*, and silver ragwort

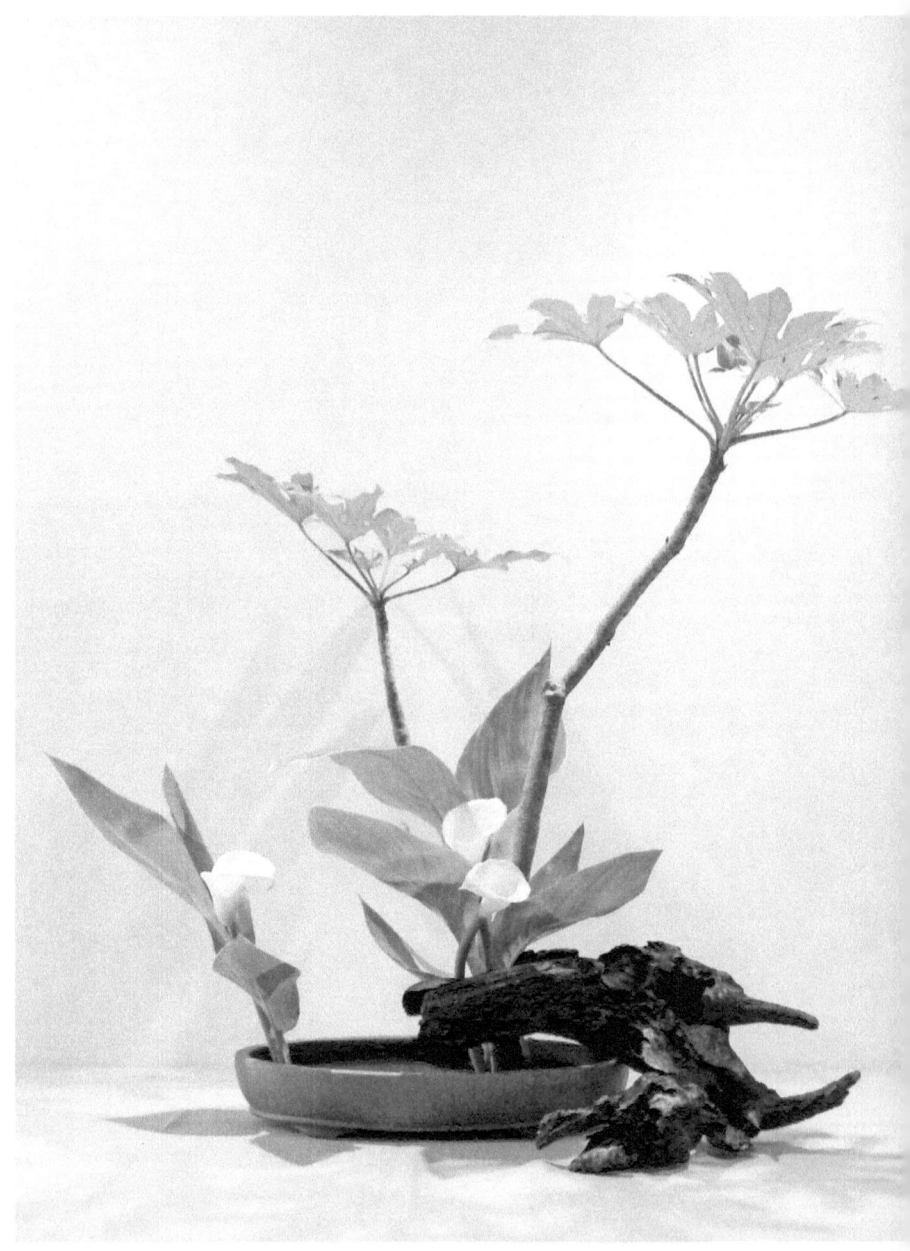

Heads Rubbing Together

Type of Arrangement	Integrated
Type of Container	Purple granulated plate
Types of Flowers	Star anise, canna, and Arum lily

Virtue of the Orchid

Type of Arrangement	Integrated
Type of Container	Pea-green vessel
Types of Flowers	*Liriope muscari 'variegata'*, *ophiopogon japoni-cus*, small white chrysanthemum, and alpine

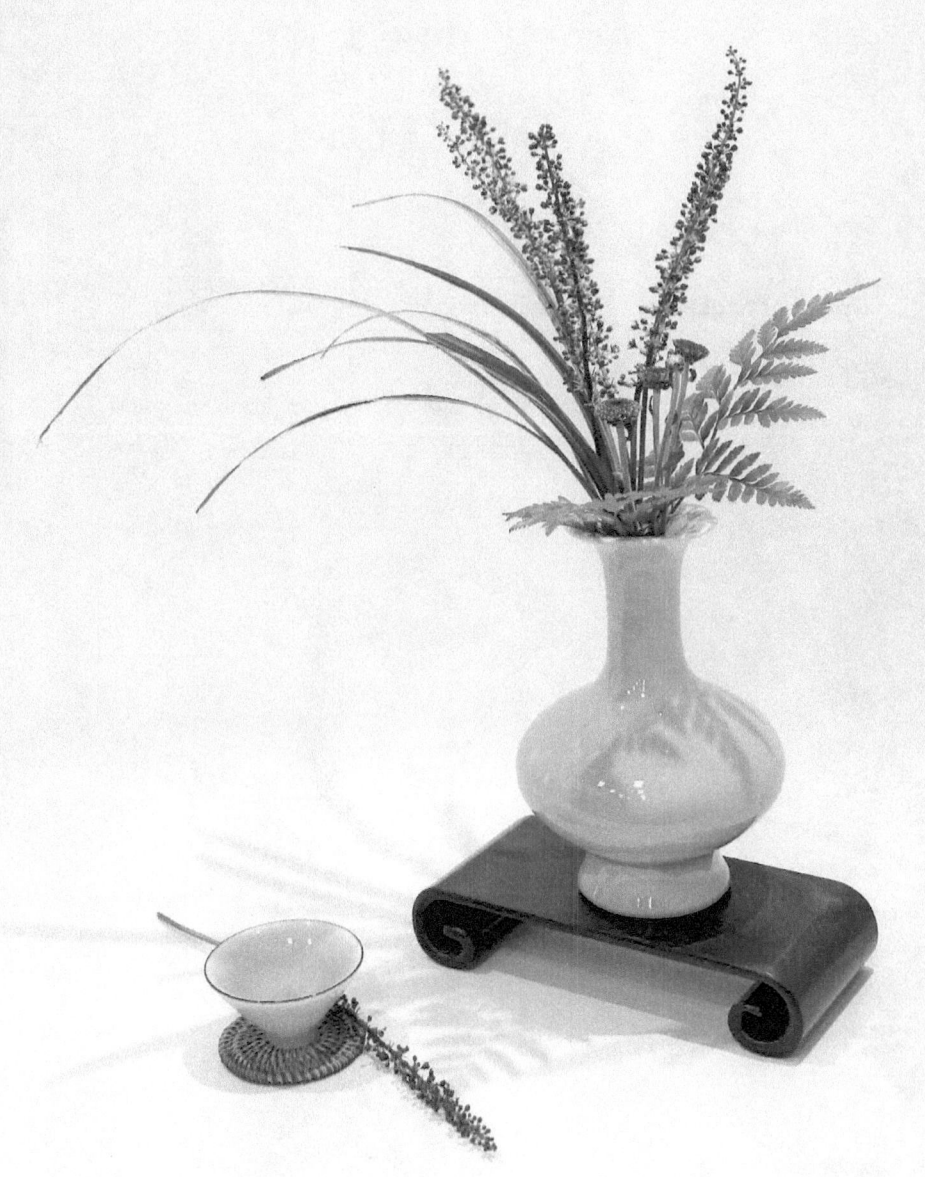

Soul Mate

Type of Arrangement	Vertically upright
Type of Container	Plastic plate
Types of Flowers	*Arum lily, photinia, farfugium japonicum,* and *ovatus aureus*

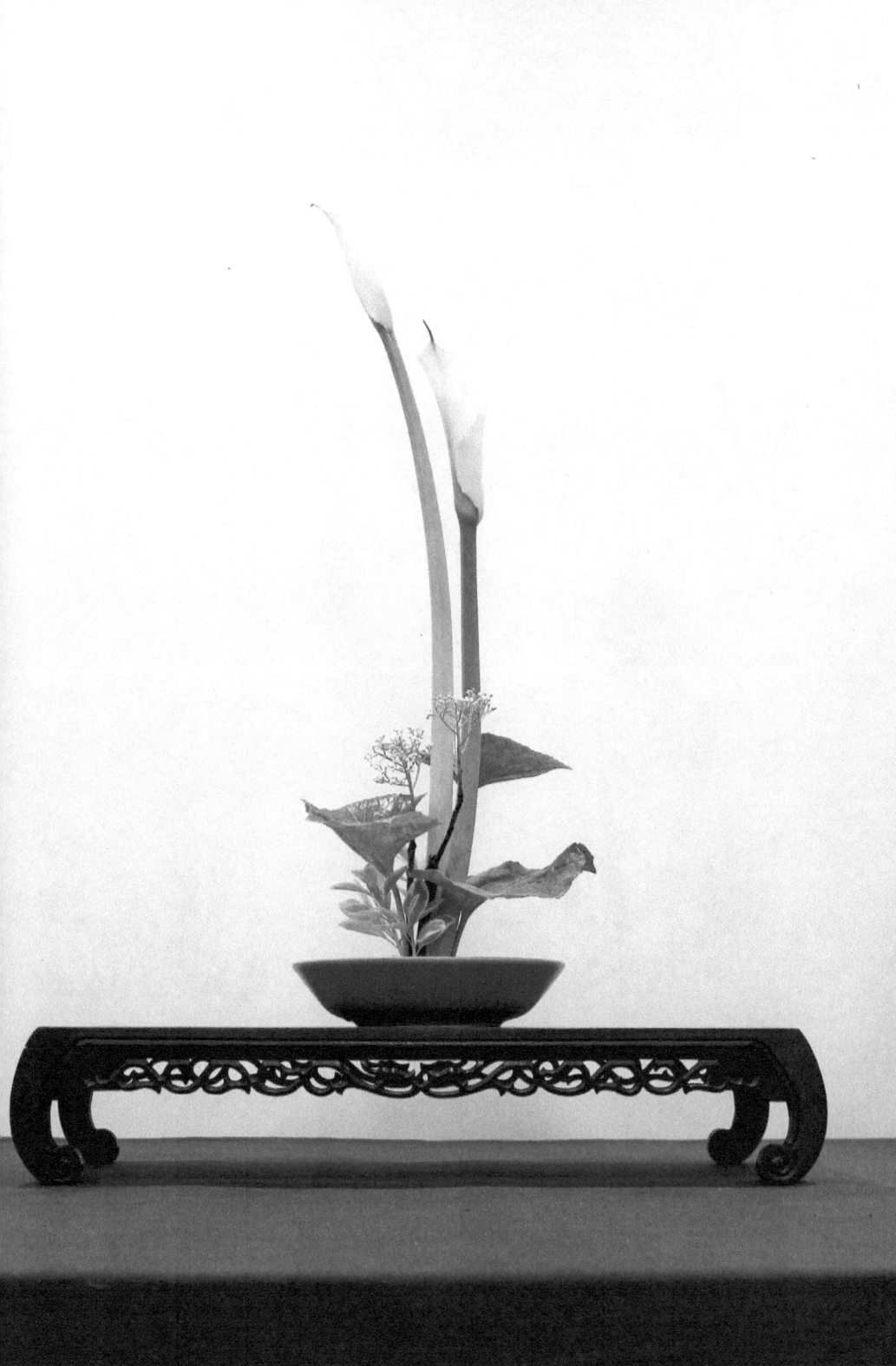

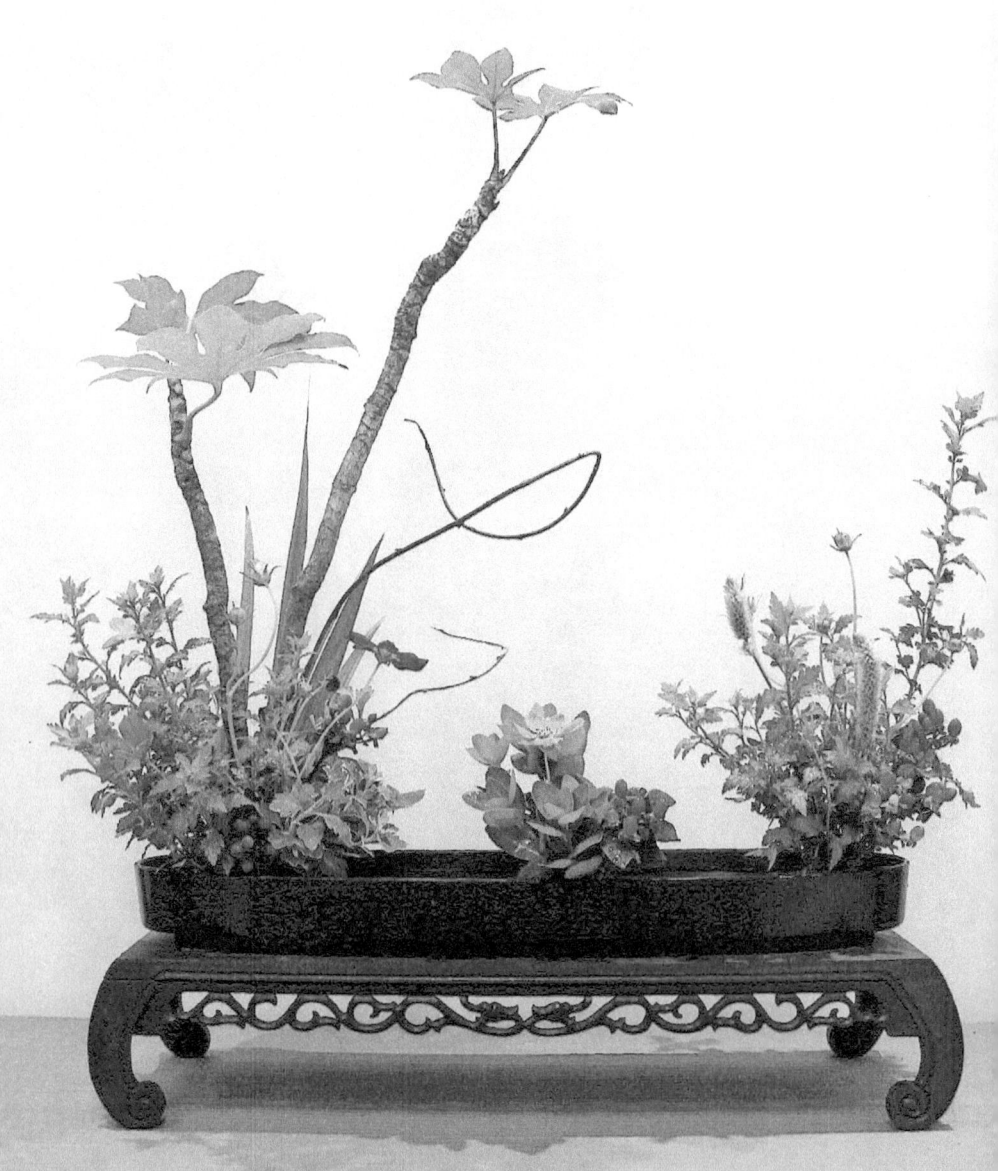

The Spring River Ravages the Flower Boat

Type of Arrangement	Integrated
Type of Container	Plastic plate
Types of Flowers	Star anise, iron lily, wild chrysanthemum, *cosmos*, *celosia argentea*, alpine, and *euonymus*

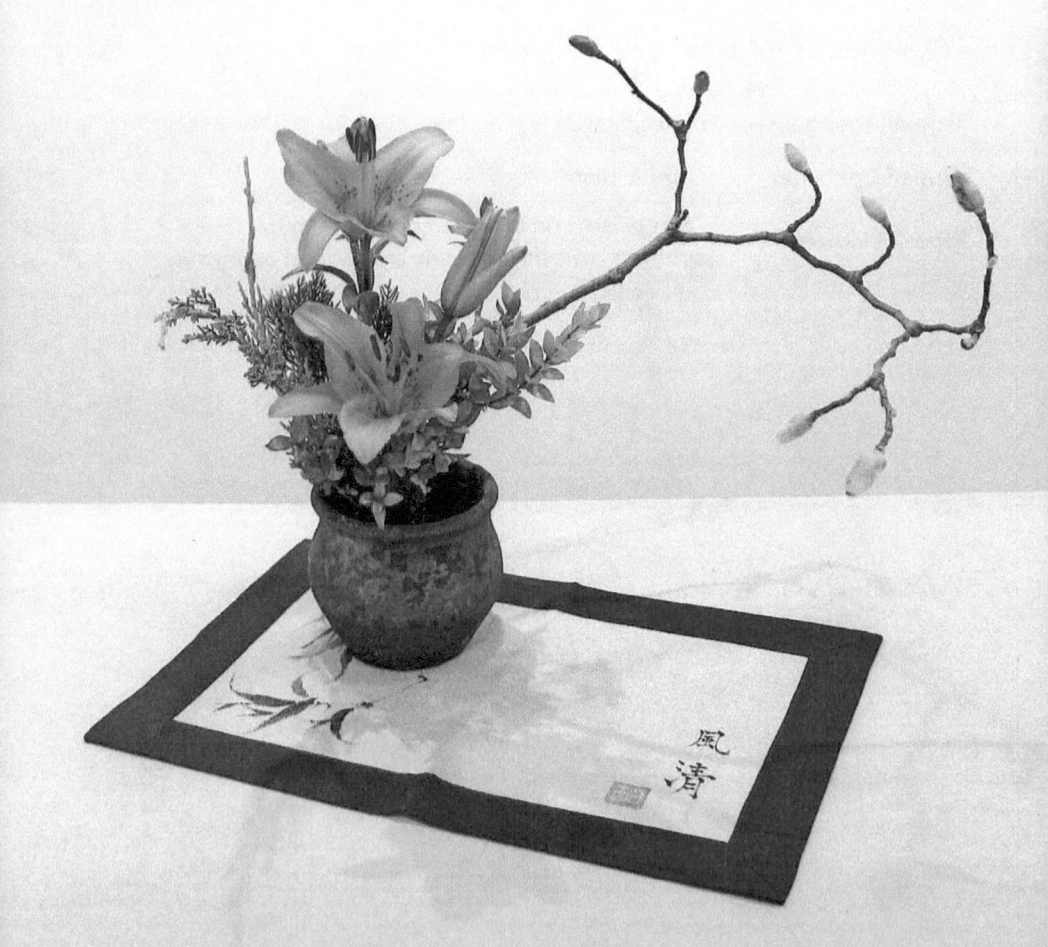

Harmonious Breeze

Type of Arrangement	Flat
Type of Container	Porcelain vase
Types of Flowers	White magnolia branches, golden lily, orange-jasmine, and alpine

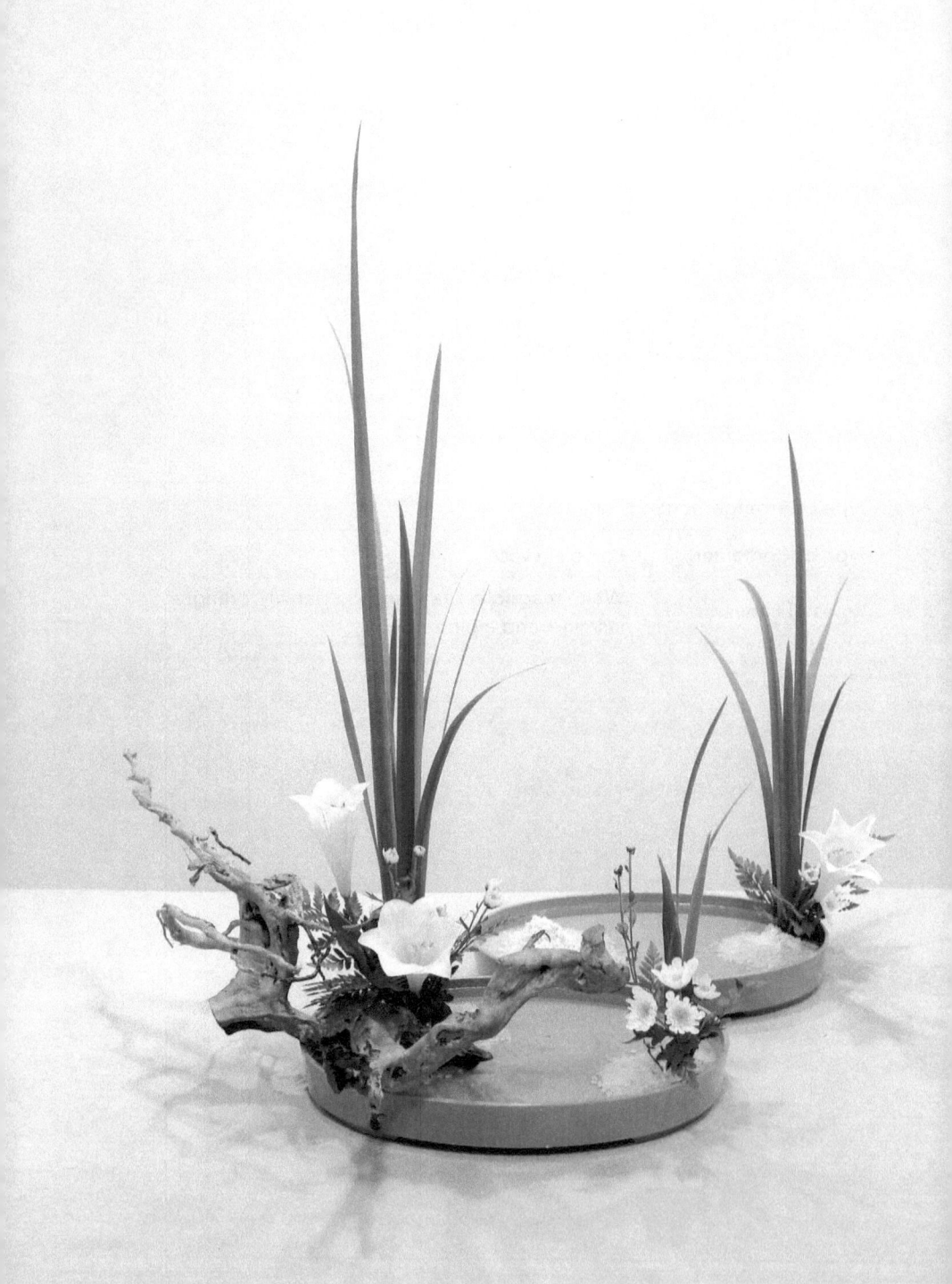

The Wind Dilutes the Shallow Pond

Type of Arrangement	Integrated
Type of Container	Plastic plate
Types of Flowers	Iris leaf, iron lily, small white chrysanthemum, and alpine

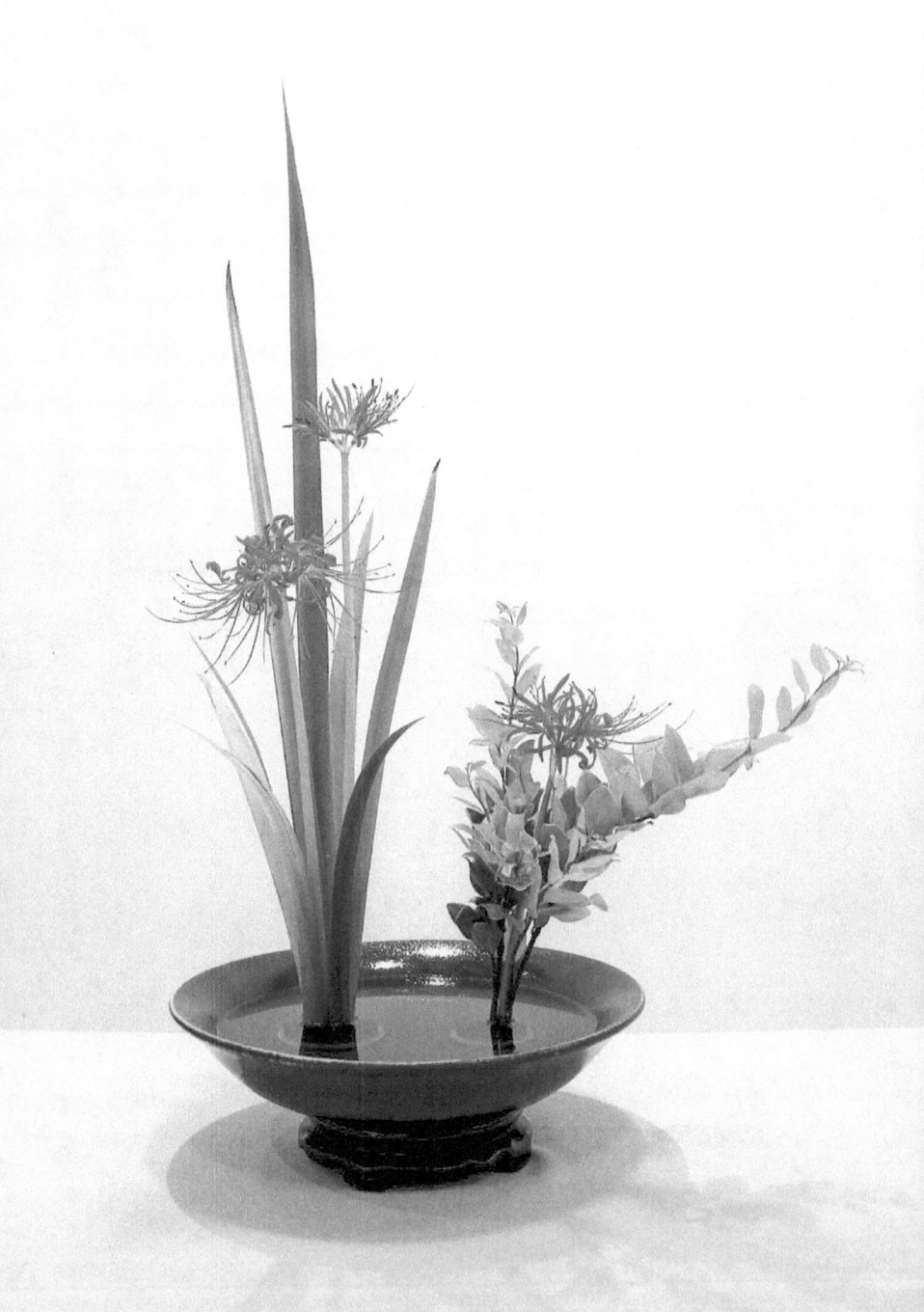

Knowing Each Other

Type of Arrangement	Integrated
Type of Container	Celadon plate
Types of Flowers	Iris leaves, red spider lily, and *ligustrum japonicum 'Howardii'*

Floating

Type of Arrangement	Integrated
Type of Container	Celadon plate
Types of Flowers	*Scirpus tabernaemontani*, powdery *thalia*, pygmy waterlily, small purple chrysanthemum, and silver ragwort

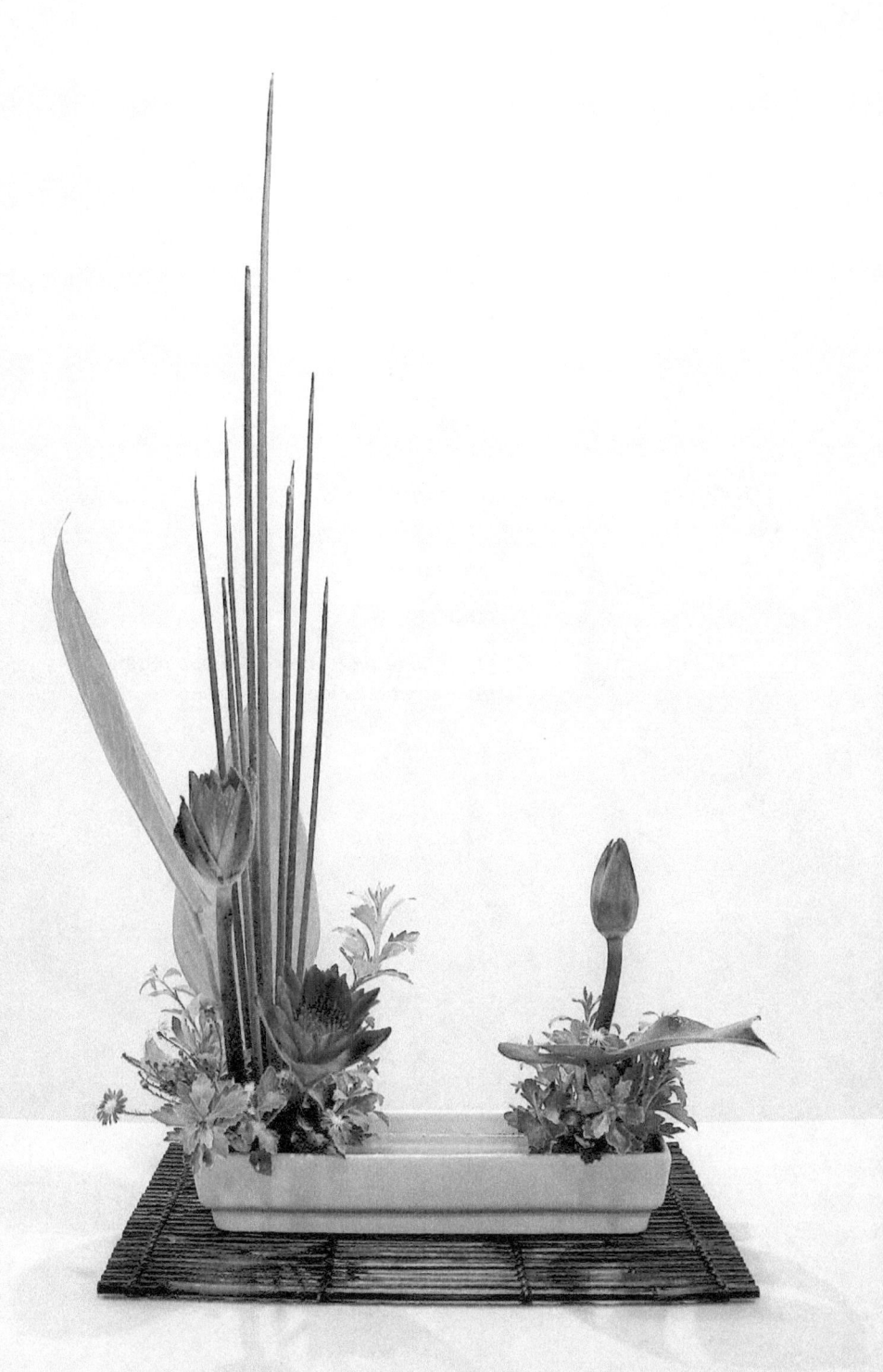

A Crane's Shadow on the Frosty Pool

Type of Arrangement	Integrated
Type of Container	Plastic plate
Types of Flowers	*Strelitzia reginae aiton, strelitzia reginae* leaf, powdery *thalia* leaf, and *coleus*

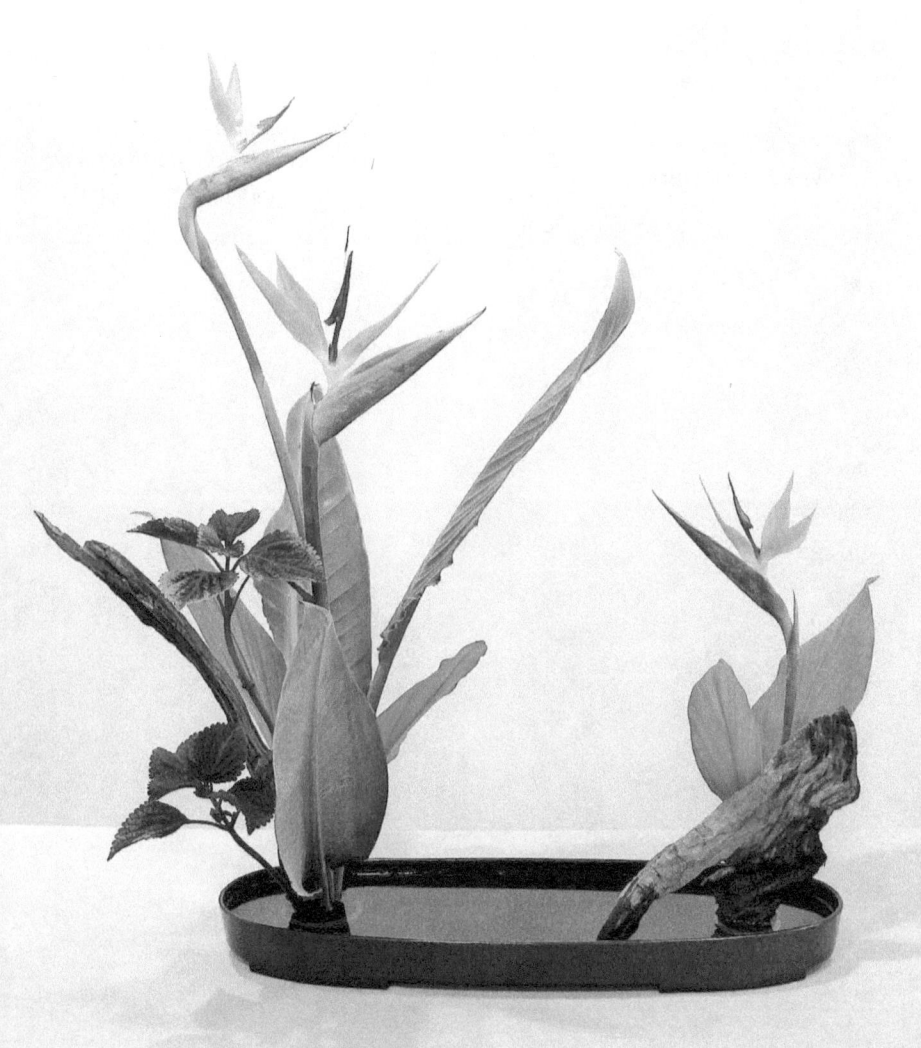

Rainbow After Rain

Type of Arrangement	Flat
Type of Container	Bamboo plate
Types of Flowers	Winter jasmine, *rhapis multifida, ganoderma ucidum, philodendron cv. xanadu,* Peruvian lily (Narcissus lily), alpine, Chinese *usnea*, and iris leaf

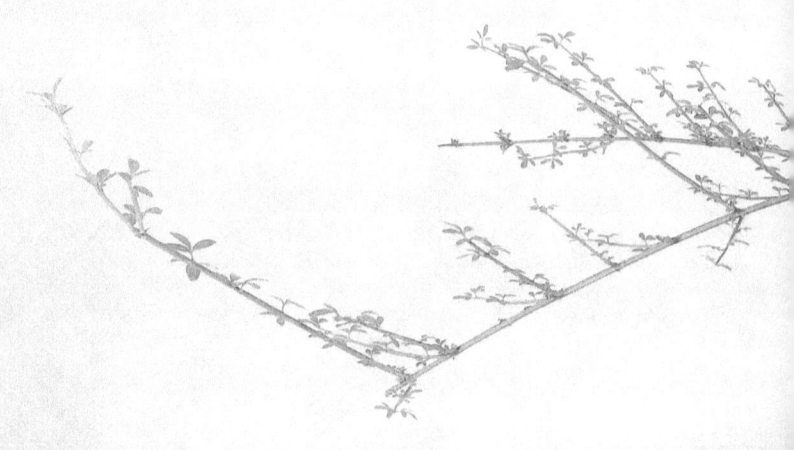

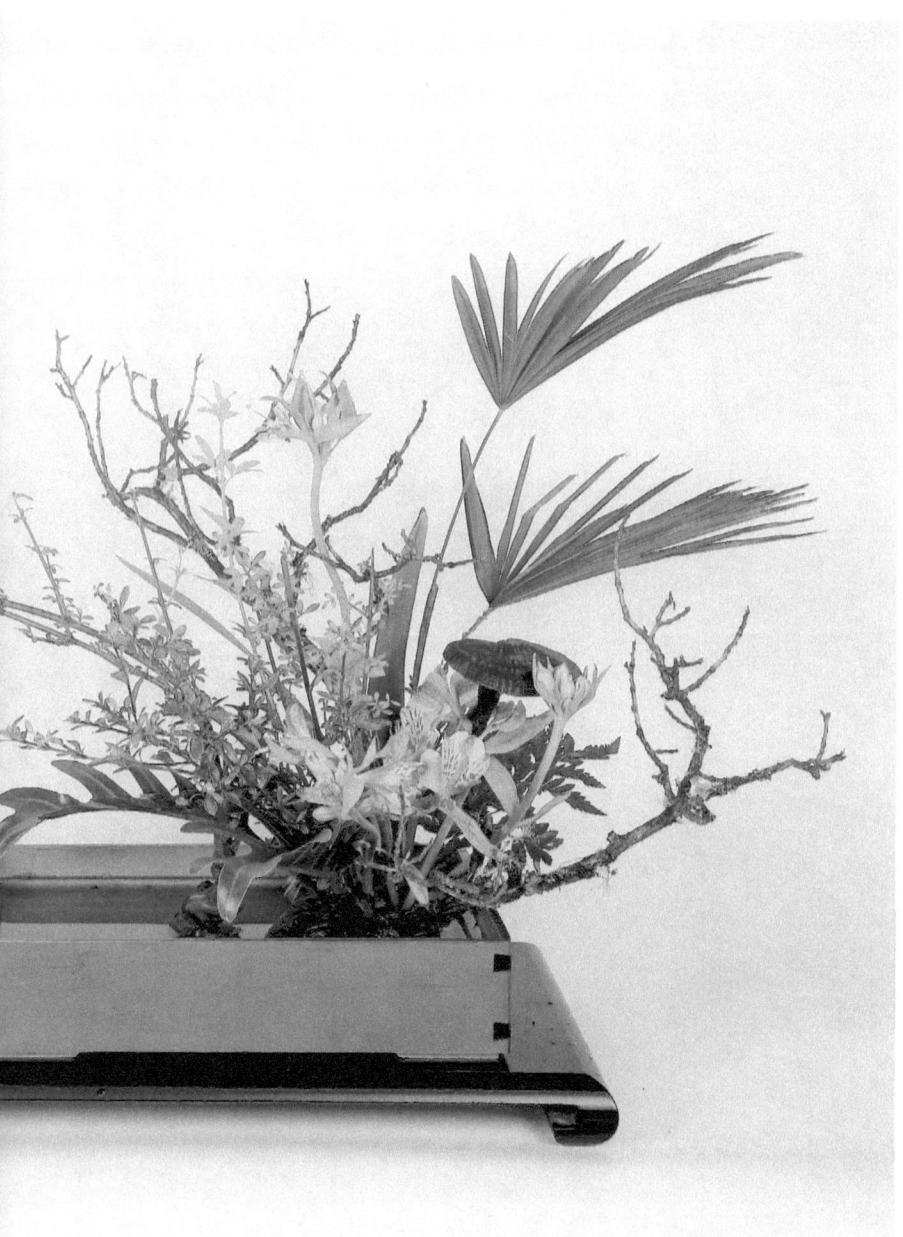

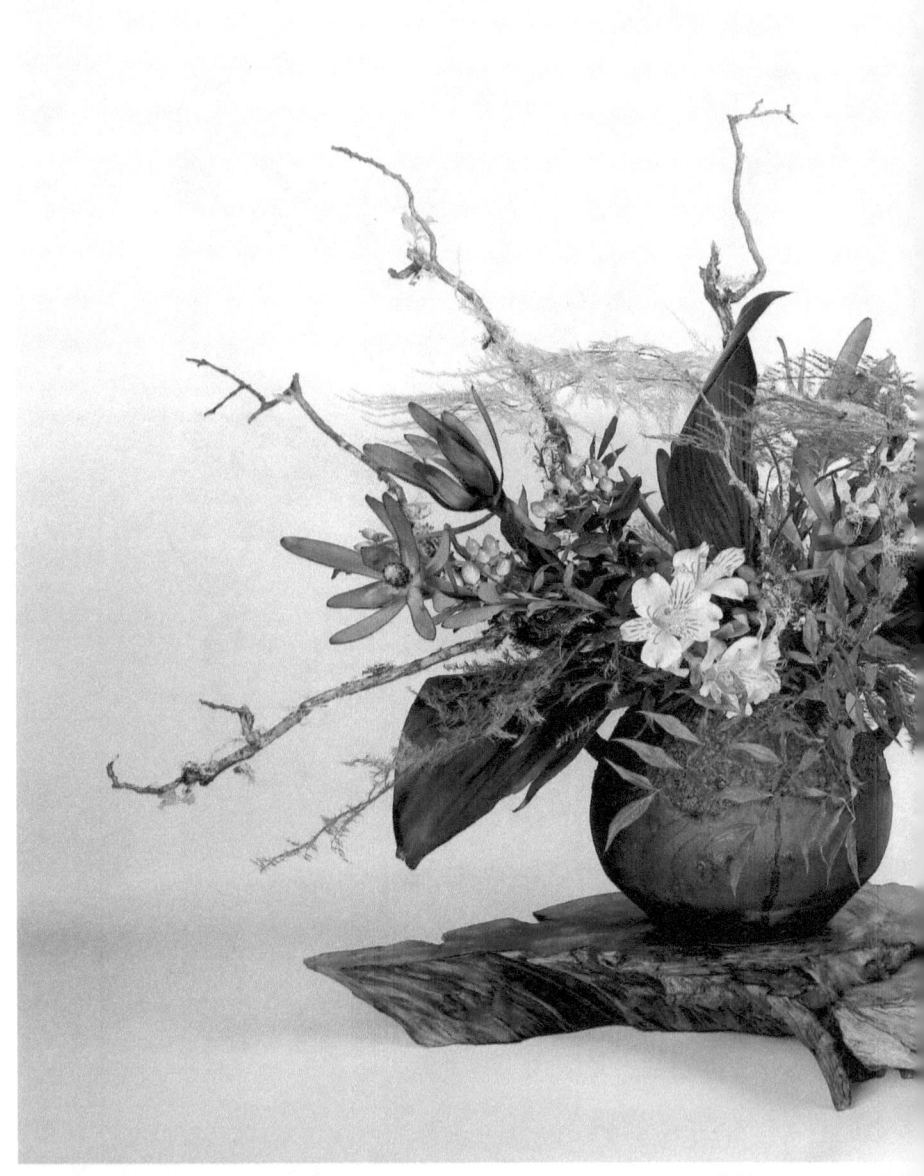

Cry of a Distant Deer

Type of Arrangement	Flat
Type of Container	Earthenware terrine
Types of Flowers	Chinese usnea, asparagus, *leucadendro*, Peruvian lily (Narcissus lily), *hypericum*, *nandina domestica*, and *canna warszewiczii*

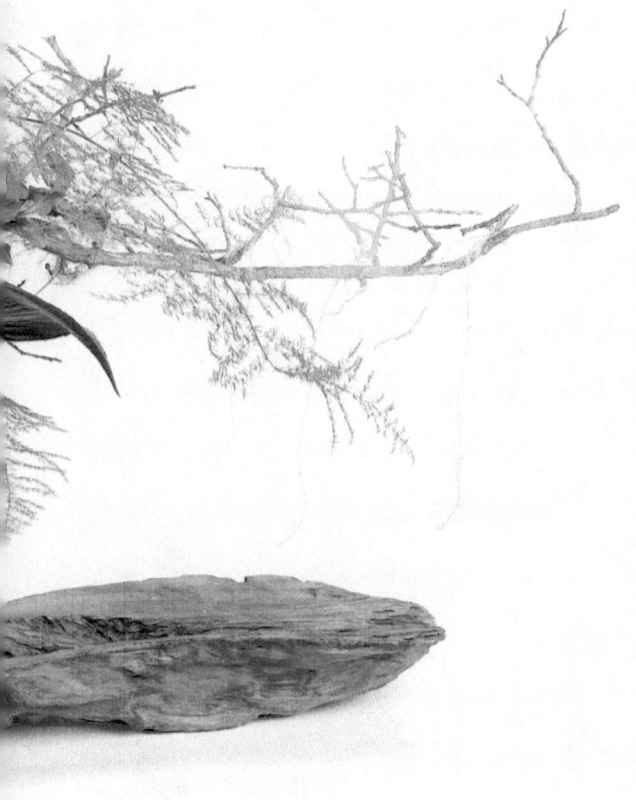

Autumn Inebriation

Type of Arrangement	Tilting
Type of Container	Porcelain flower goblet
Types of Flowers	*leucadendro*, Indian pokeweed, rosehip, and alpine

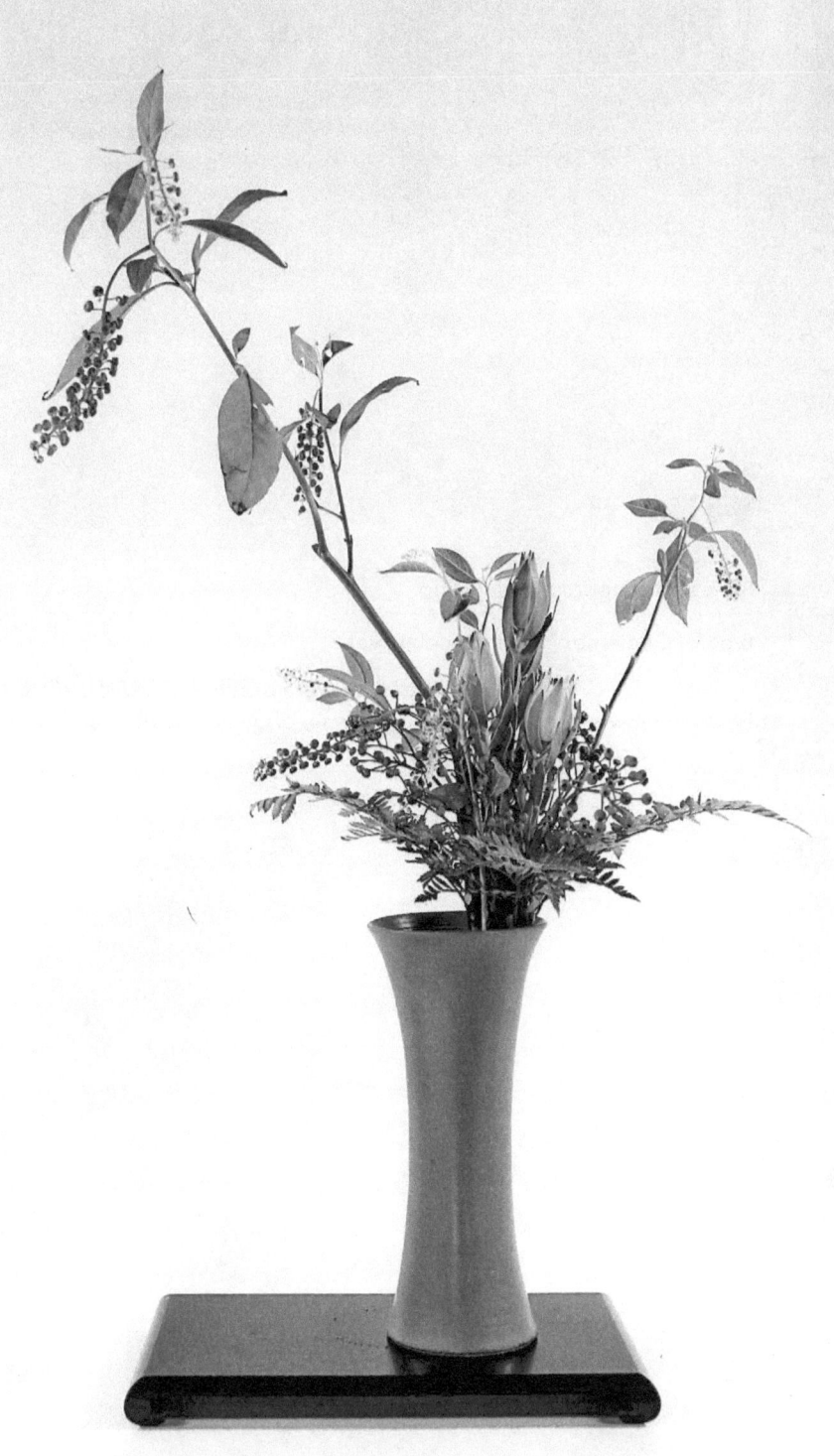

Web of Deceit

Type of Arrangement	Tilting
Type of Container	Porcelain vase
Types of Flowers	Cypress, *goodyera procera, aspidistra elatior, strelitzia reginae, photinia fraseri,* and Chinese wisteria

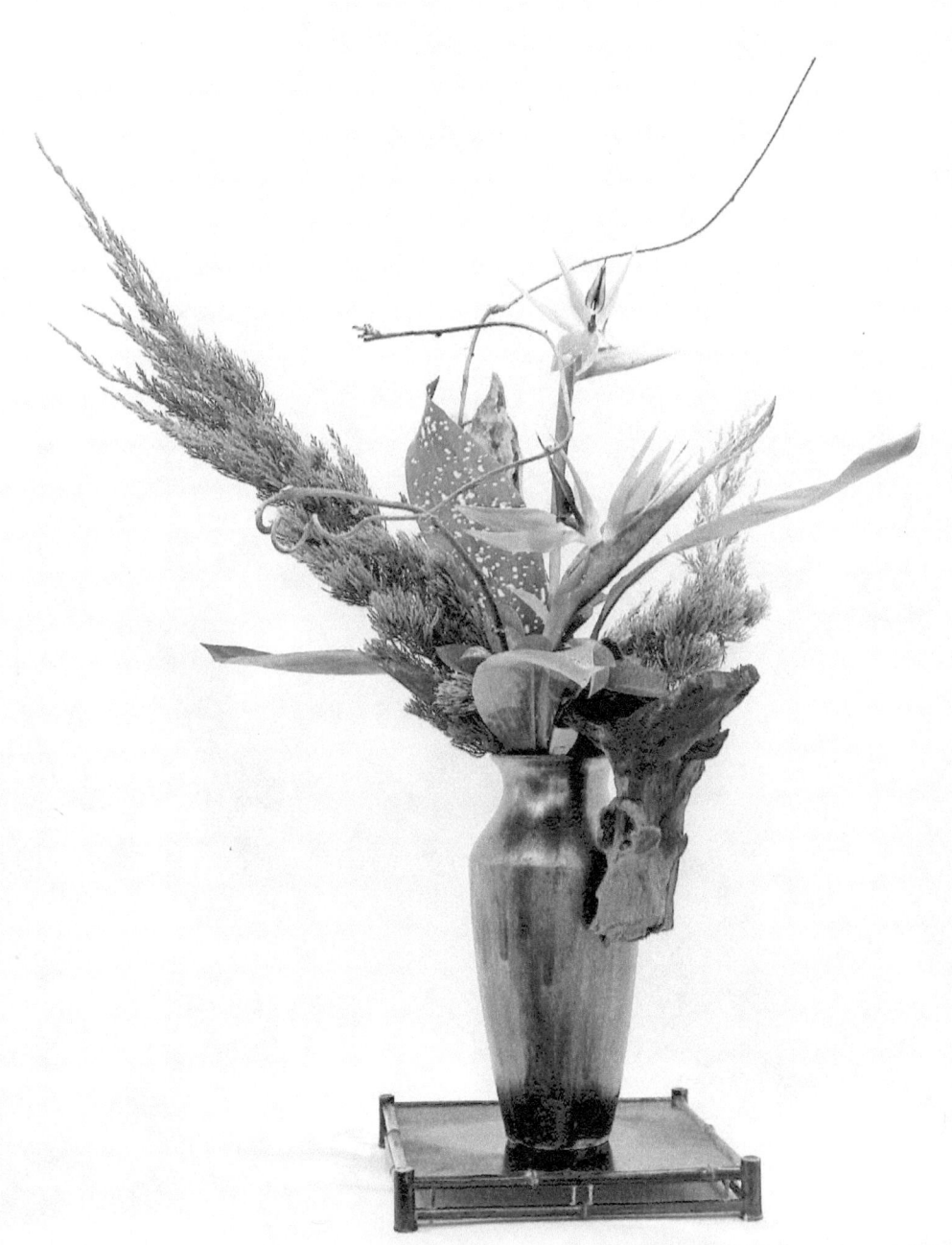

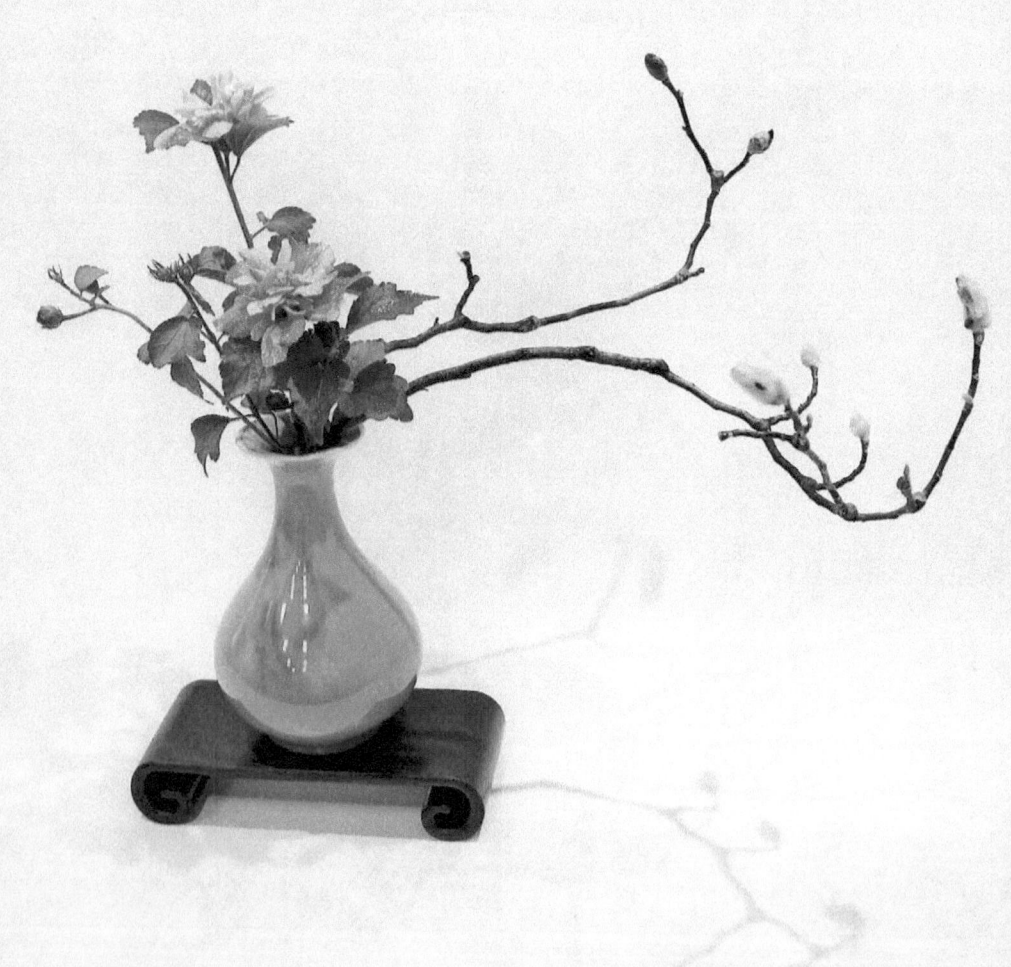

Desolate Wind

Type of Arrangement	Flat
Type of Container	Azure-blue vase
Types of Flowers	White magnolia branches and hibiscus

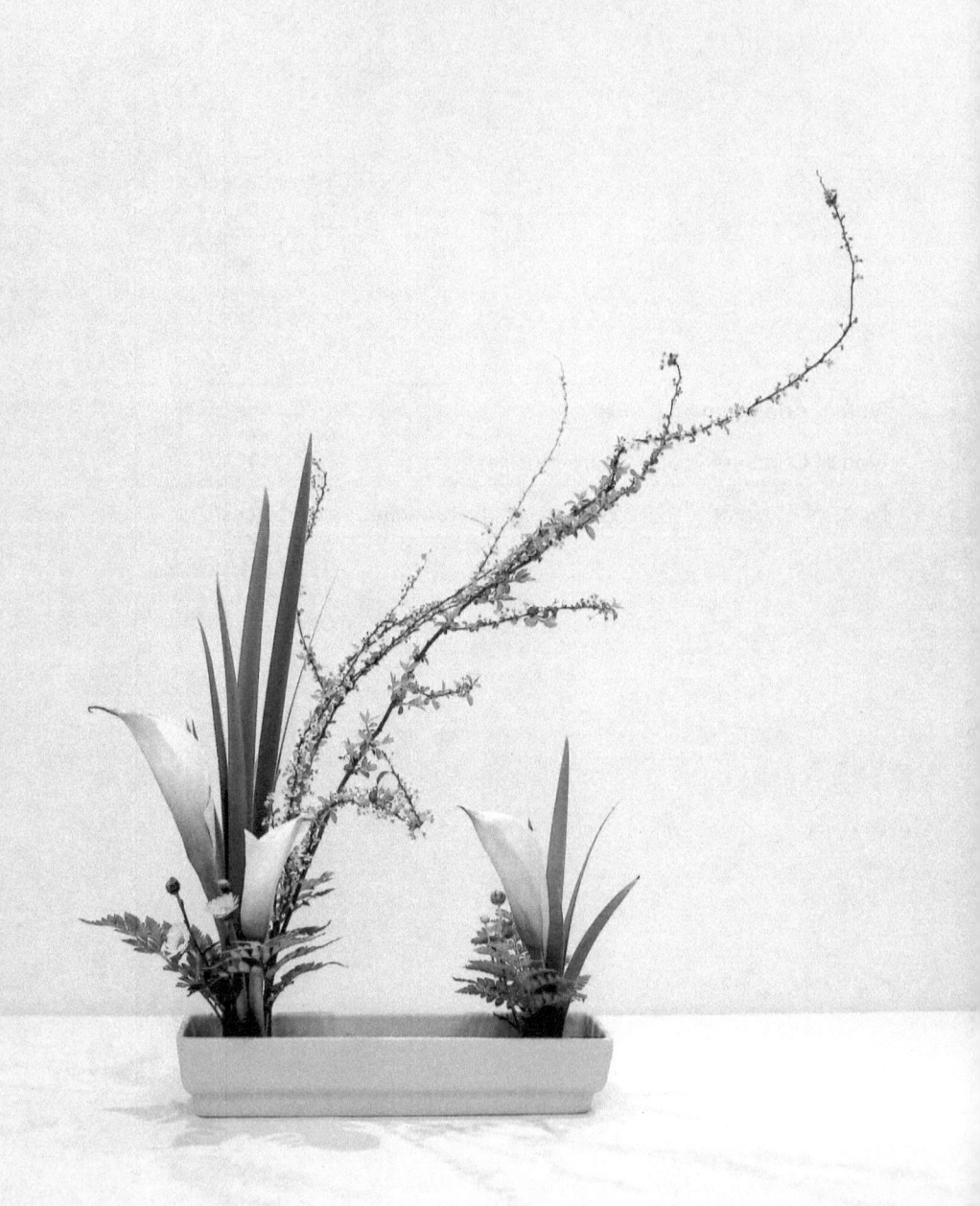

Sound of Snow

Type of Arrangement	Integrated
Type of Container	Celadon plate
Types of Flowers	Hoary willow, iris leaf, Arum lily, small purple chrysanthemum, and alpine

Resting on a Red Leaf

Type of Arrangement	Tilting
Type of Container	Celadon lamp
Types of Flowers	Red maple, pot mum, and alpine

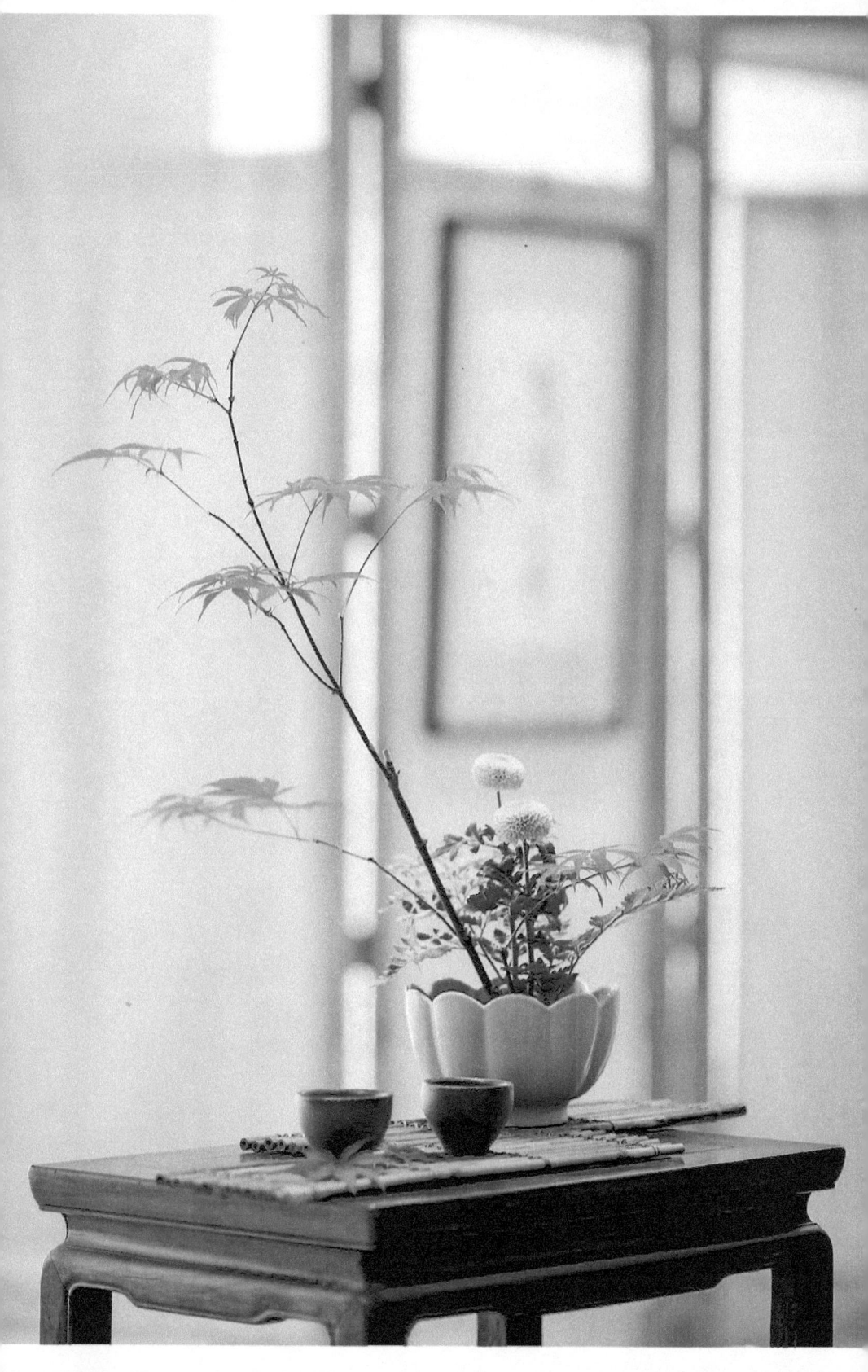

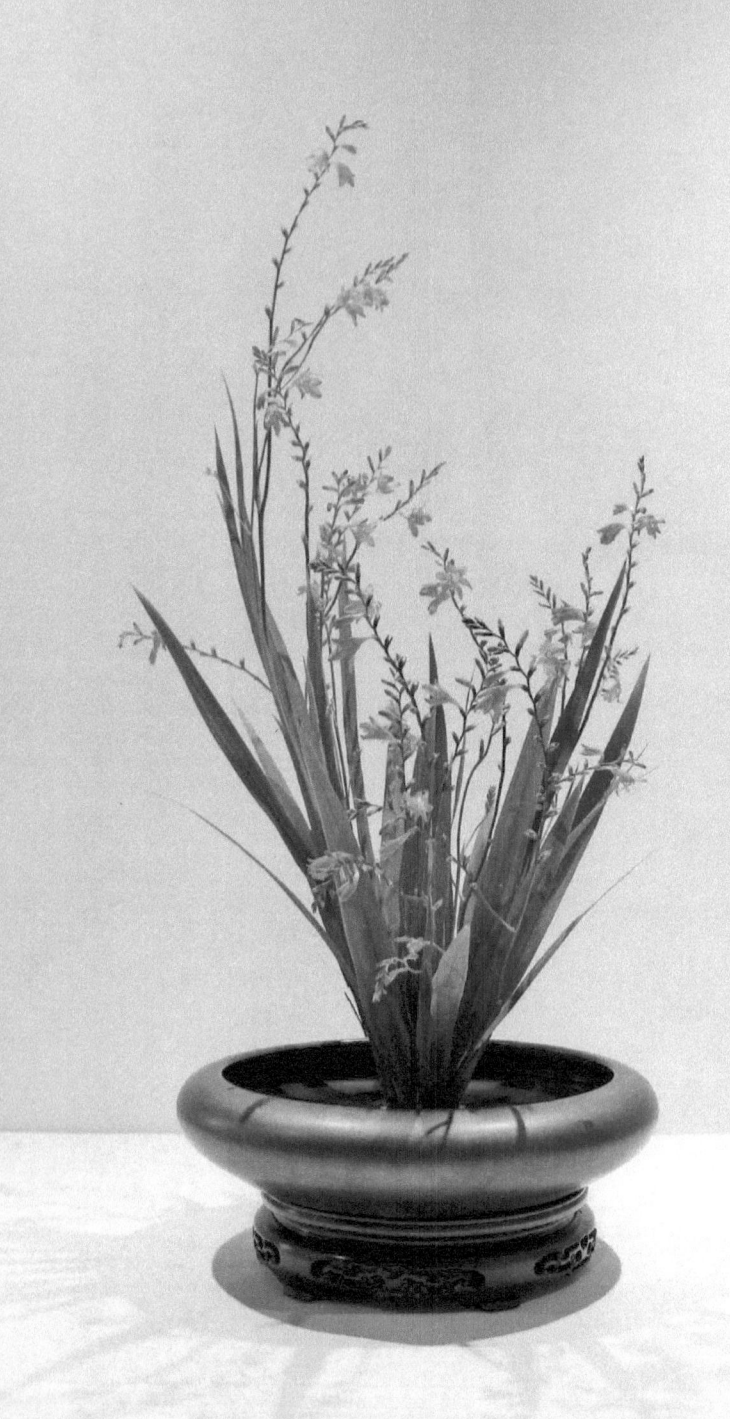

Spark

Type of Arrangement	Vertically upright
Type of Container	Ceramic pottery
Types of Flowers	*Crocosmia crocosmiflora*

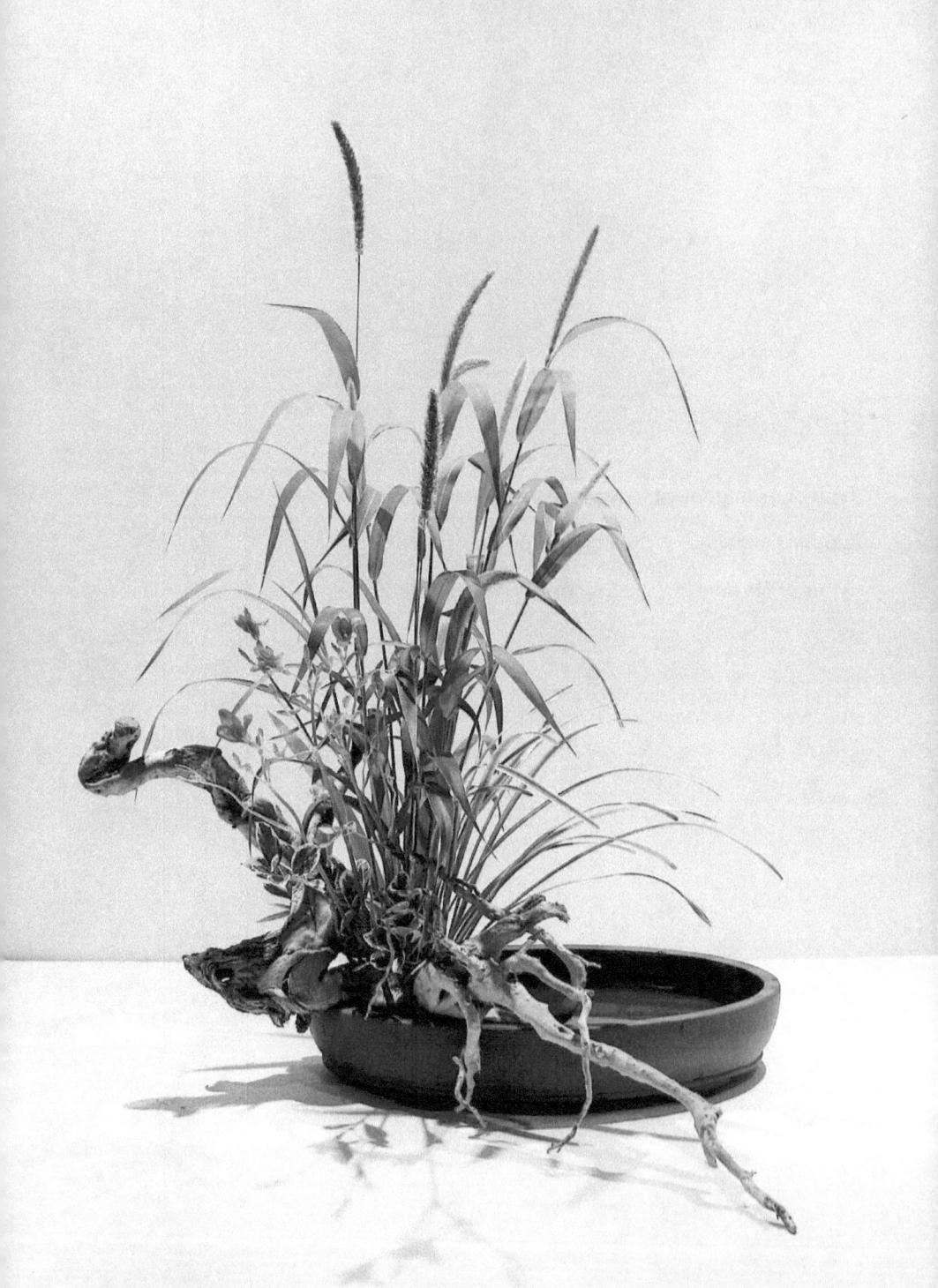

Folk Songs

Type of Arrangement	Vertically upright
Type of Container	Granulated purple plate
Types of Flowers	Blackberry lily, millet, *liriope muscari 'variegata'*, and *ovatus aureus*

Carrying the Boat

Type of Arrangement	Integrated
Type of Container	Long plastic plate
Types of Flowers	Reed catkins, water wax leaf, powdery *thalia*, Barberton daisy, French marigold, and silver ragwort

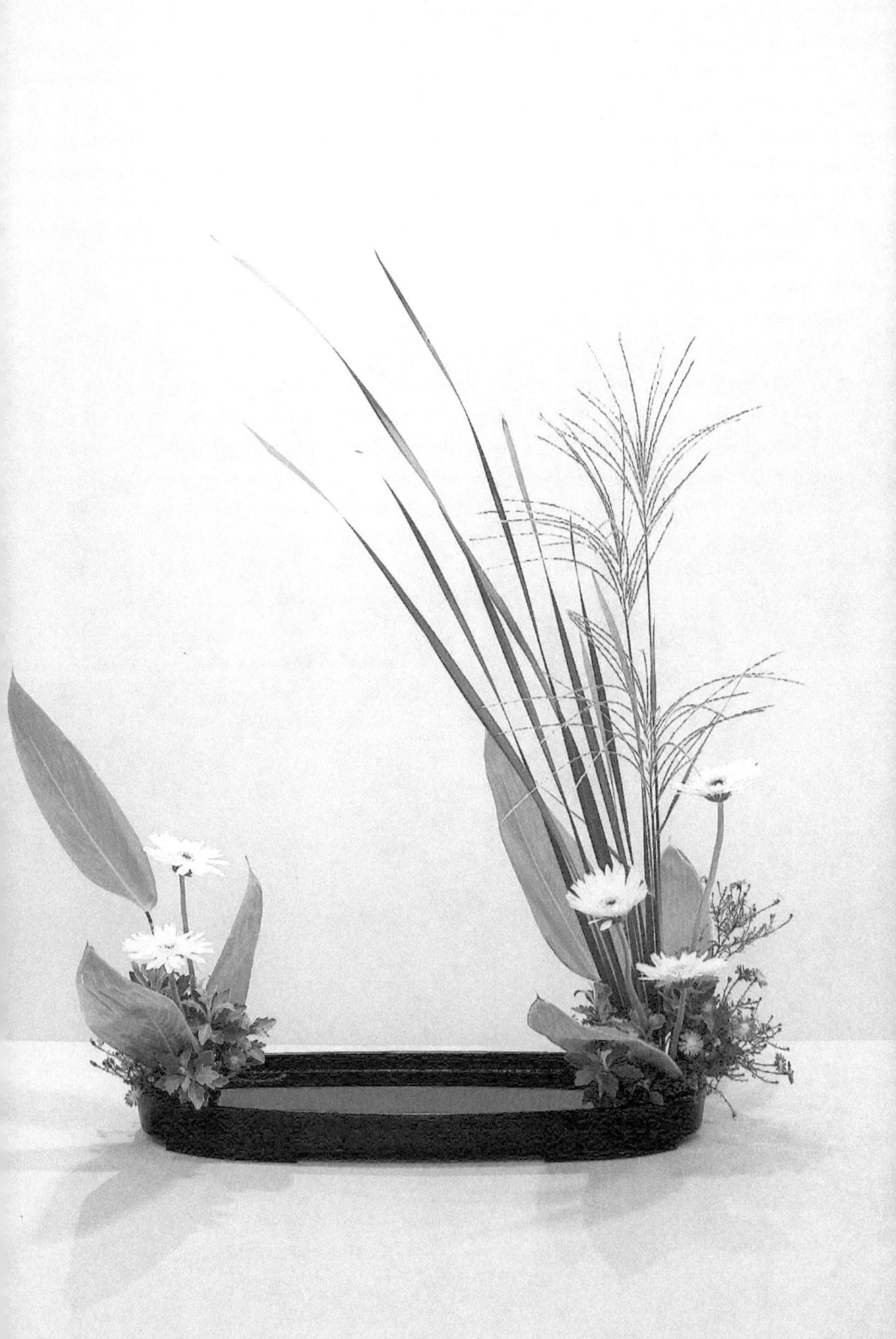

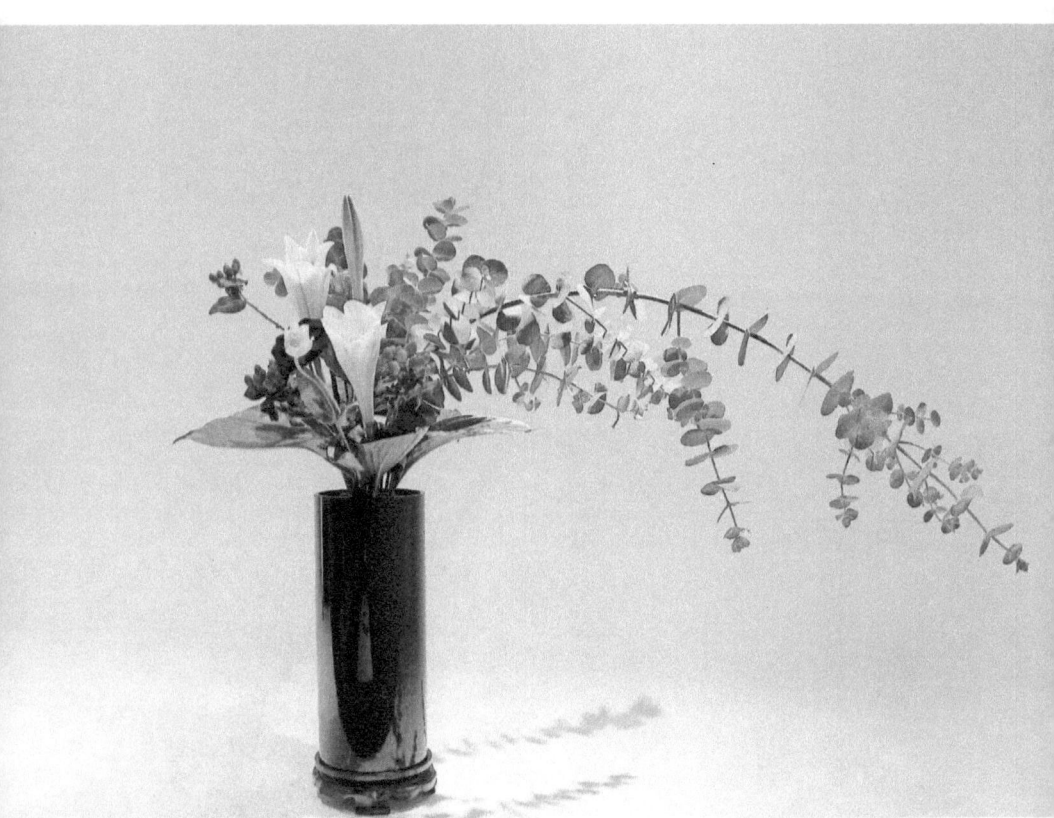

Crooning

Type of Arrangement	Flat
Type of Container	Glass tube
Types of Flowers	Hoary willow, iron lily, *hypericum*, *lisianthus*, and silver ragwort

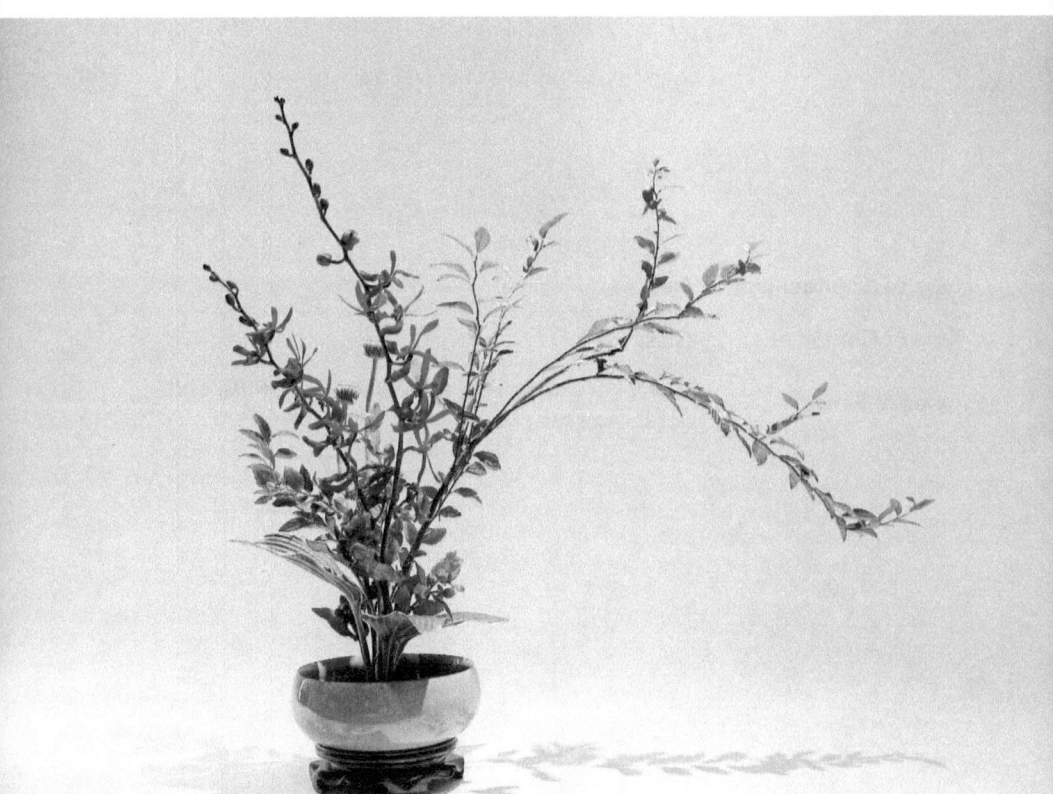

Dreams of Grandeur

Type of Arrangement	Integrated
Type of Container	Long plastic plate
Types of Flowers	Hoary willow, *vanda, hypericum,* Barberton daisy, and silver ragwort

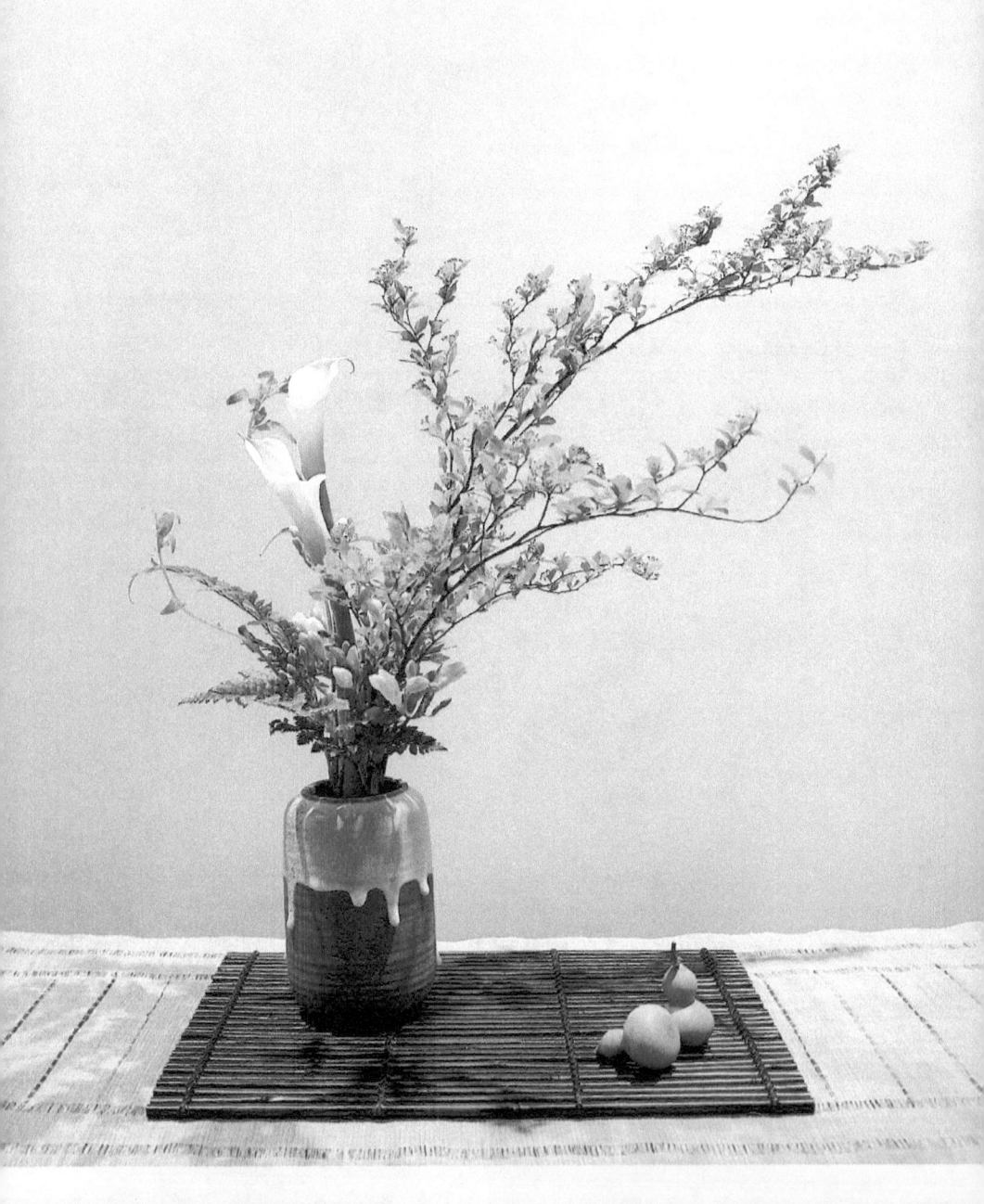

Hearing News

Type of Arrangement	Tilting
Type of Container	Ceramic can
Types of Flowers	*Spirae*, Arum lily, *freesia refracta,* and alpine

Arrival of Spring

Type of Arrangement	Tilting
Type of Container	Celadon plate
Types of Flowers	Red plum, Arum lily, and iris leaf

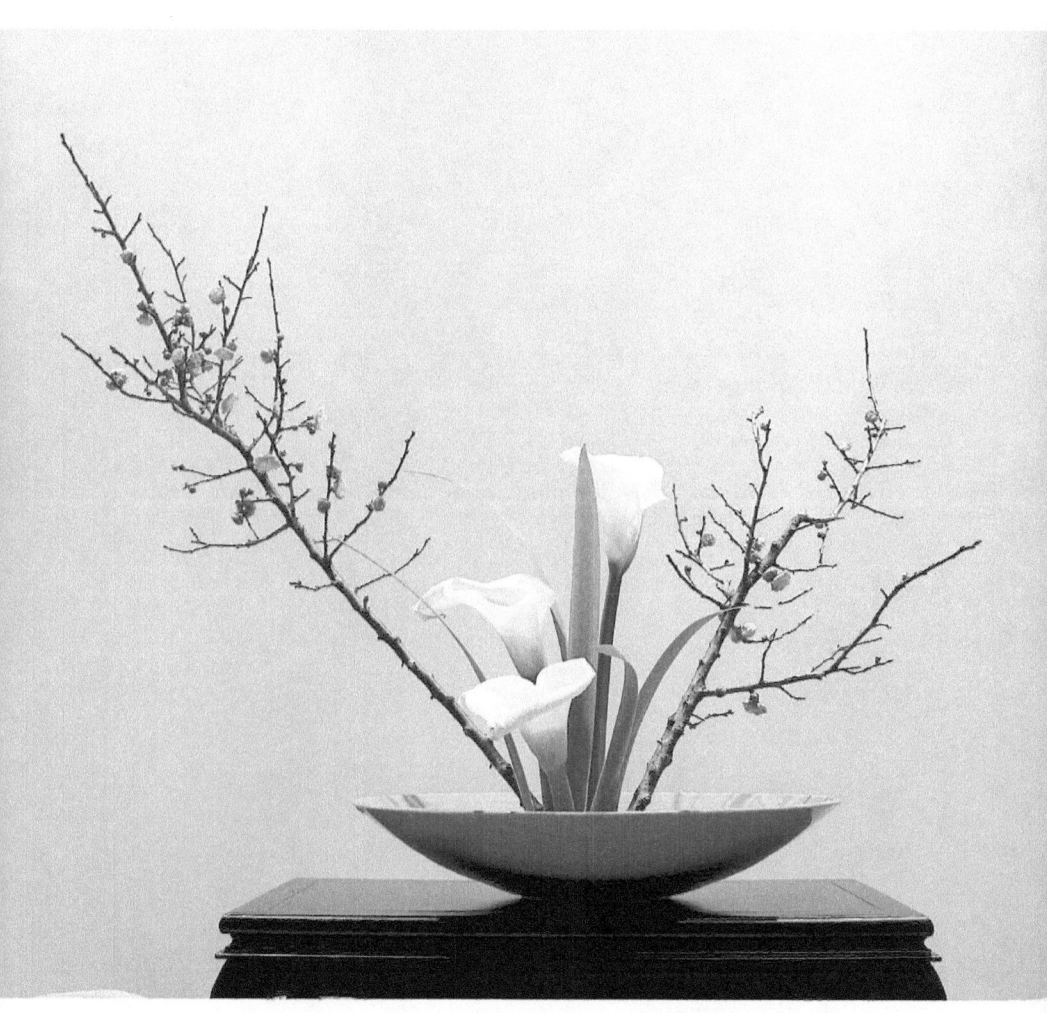

Red Snow

Type of Arrangement	Tilting
Type of Container	Bowl
Types of Flowers	Red plum, white buttercup, and *podocarpus*

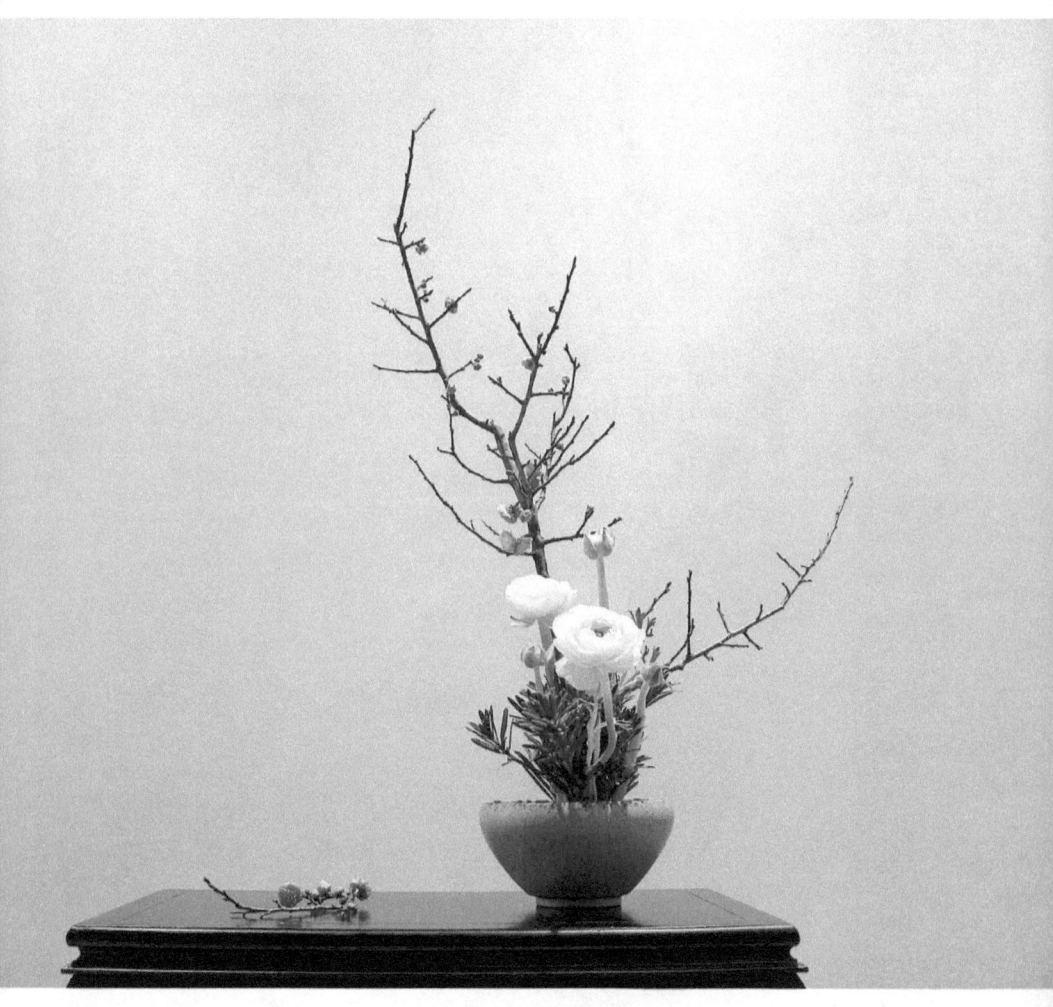

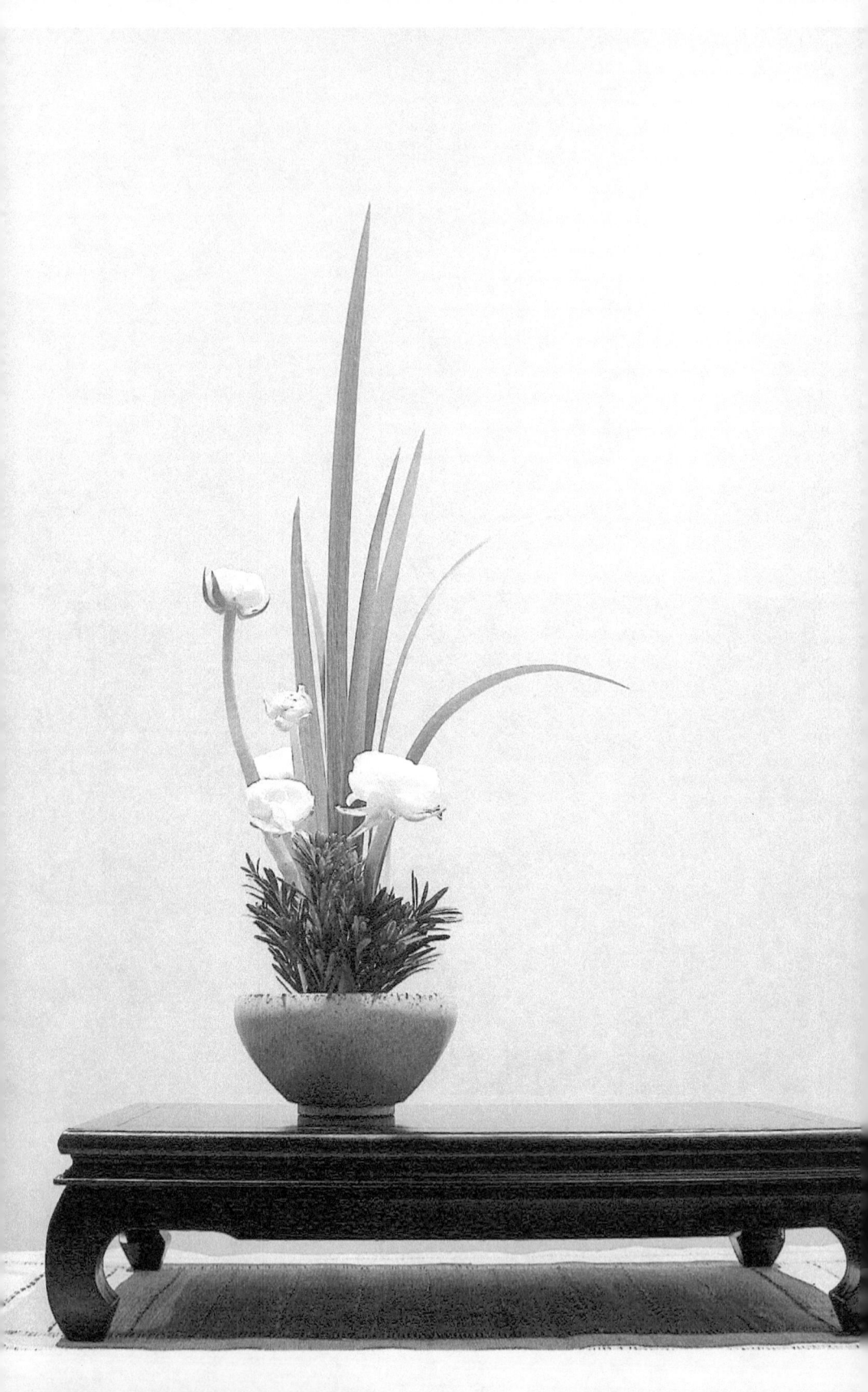

Breeze

Type of Arrangement	Vertically upright
Type of Container	Ceramic Bowl
Types of Flowers	Iris leaf, white buttercup, and *podocarpus*

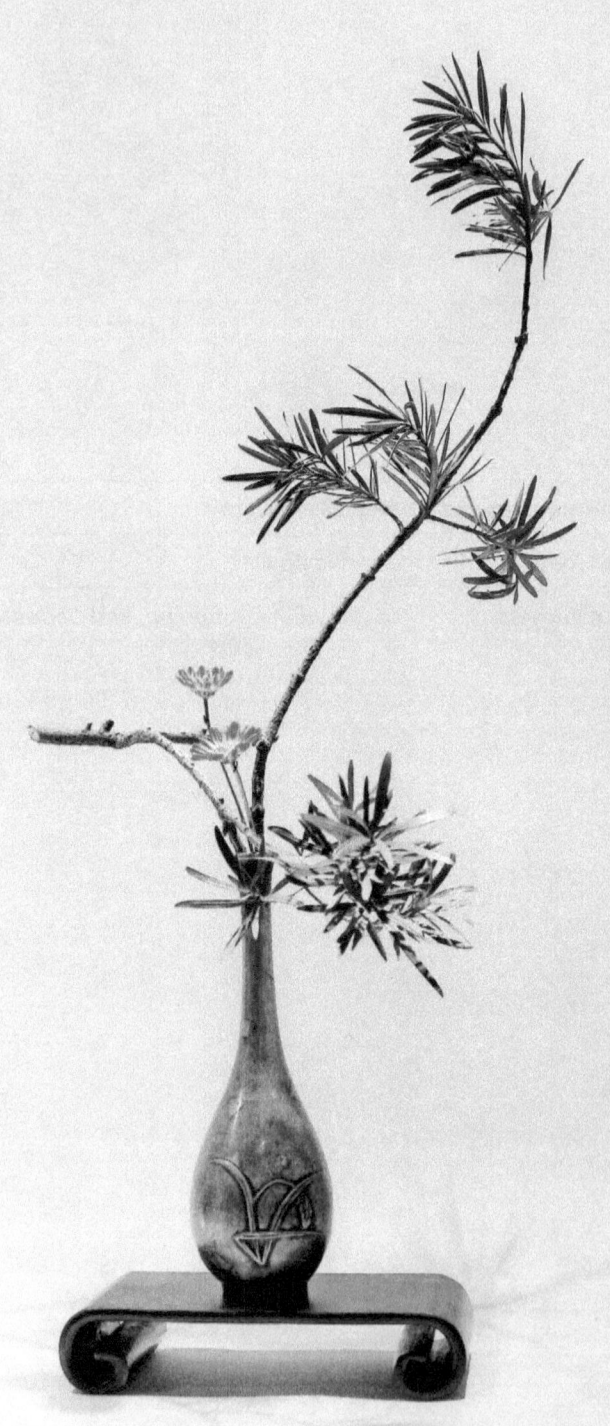

Wind in the High Pine

Type of Arrangement	Tilting
Type of Container	Copper dish
Types of Flowers	*Podocarpus* and small orange chrysanthemum

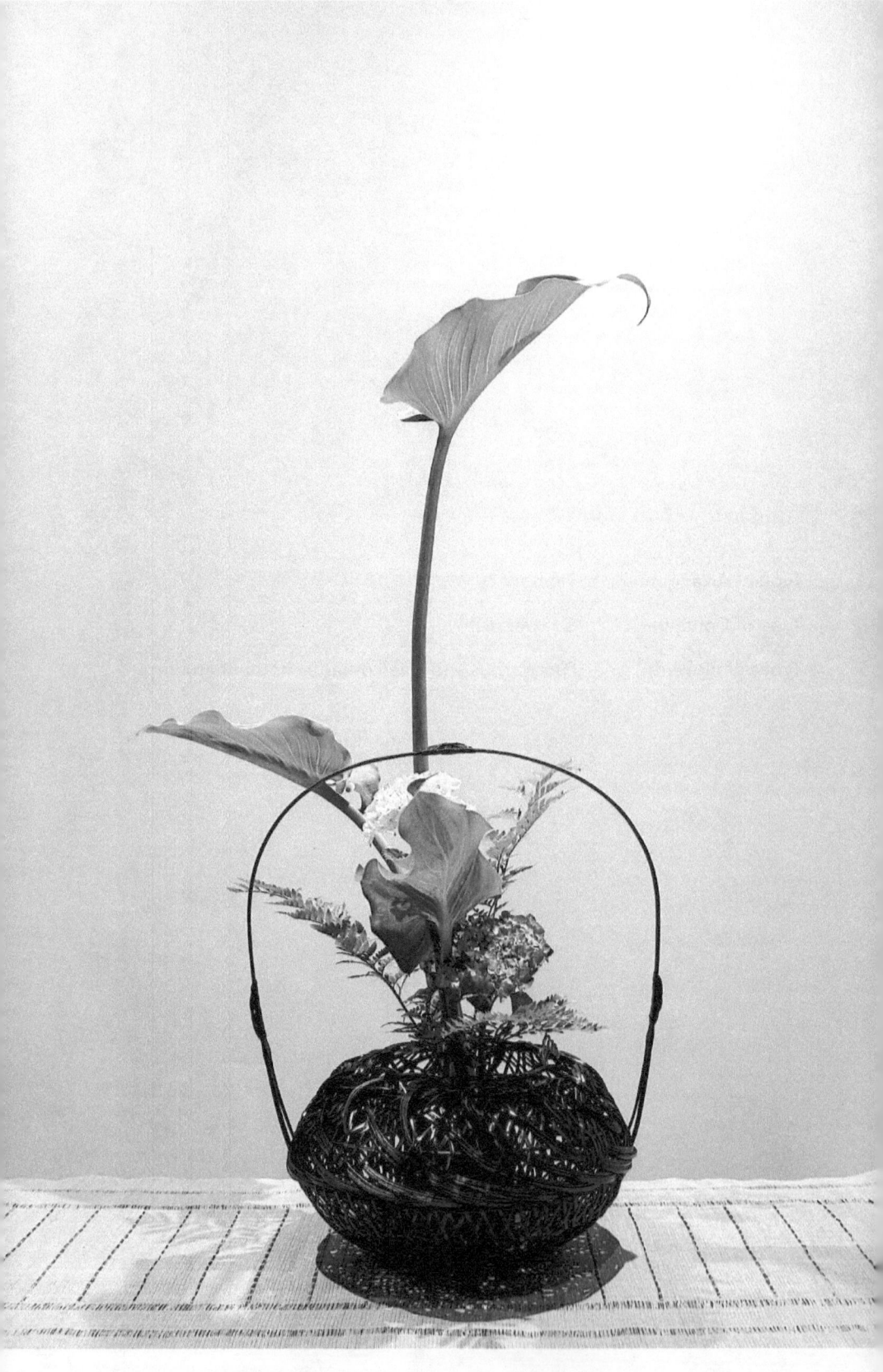

Raindrops from the Heart

Type of Arrangement	Vertically upright
Type of Container	Bamboo basket
Types of Flowers	*Hydrangea macrophylla*, Arum lily, and alpine

Cloud Peak

Type of Arrangement	Vertically upright
Type of Container	Porcelain plate
Types of Flowers	Dead wood, wisteria, pod leaves, and small white chrysanthemum

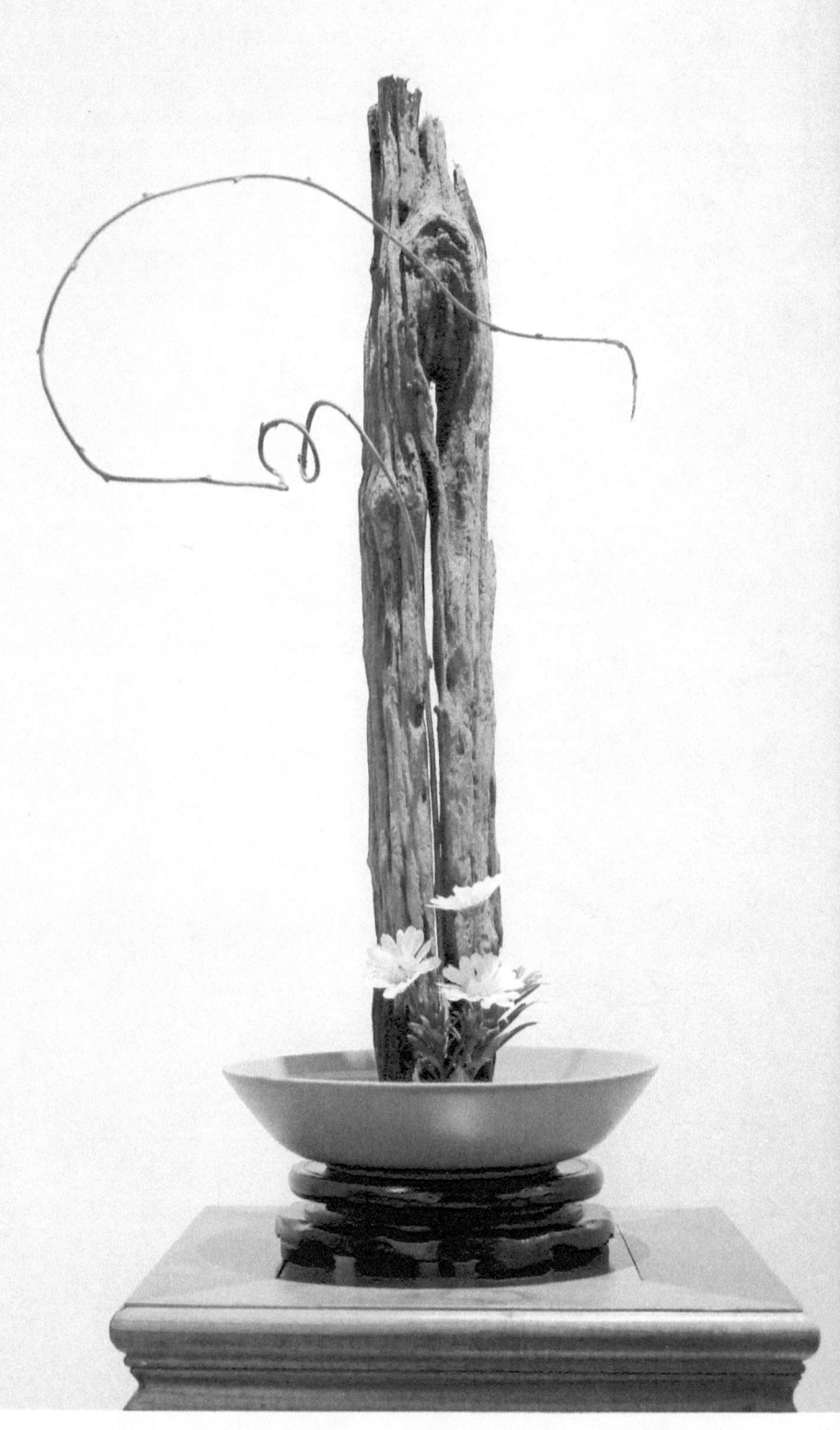

Meeting

Type of Arrangement	Integrated
Type of Container	Lacquer box
Types of Flowers	Red spider lily, orange-jasmine, silver ragwort, and small purple chrysanthemum

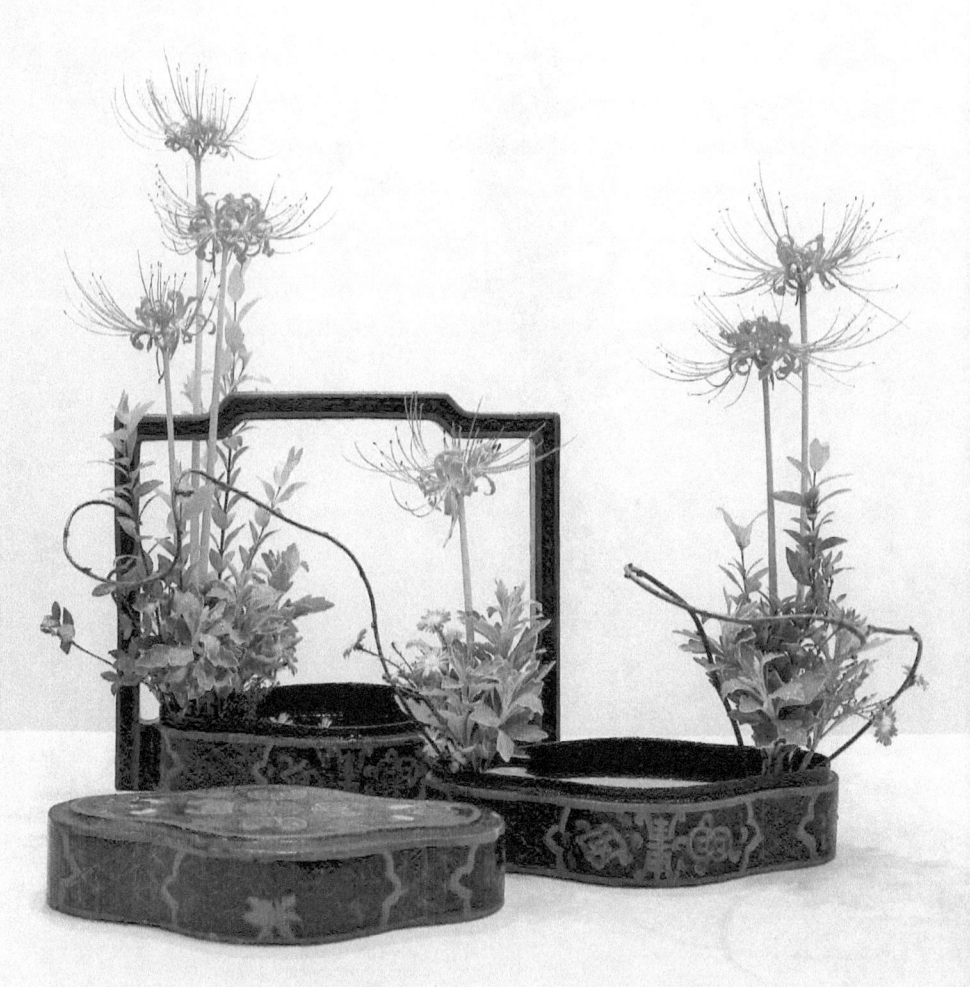

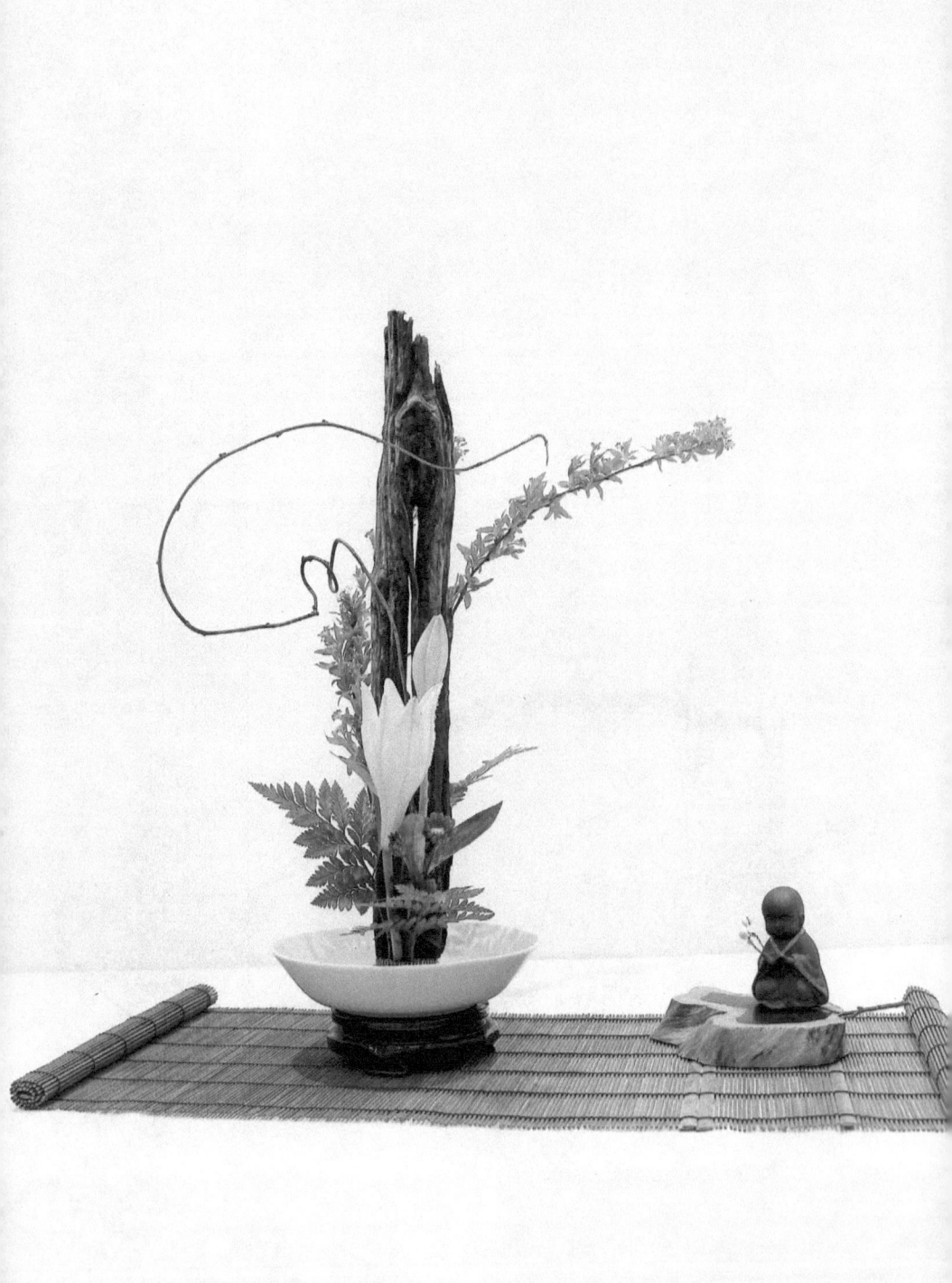

Heart Sutra

Type of Arrangement	Vertically upright
Type of Container	Porcelain plate
Types of Flowers	Hoary willow, iron lily, small red chrysanthemum, and alpine

Dawn

Type of Arrangement	Tilting
Type of Container	Ceramic pottery
Types of Flowers	Hoary willow, iron lily, small pink chrysanthemum, and alpine

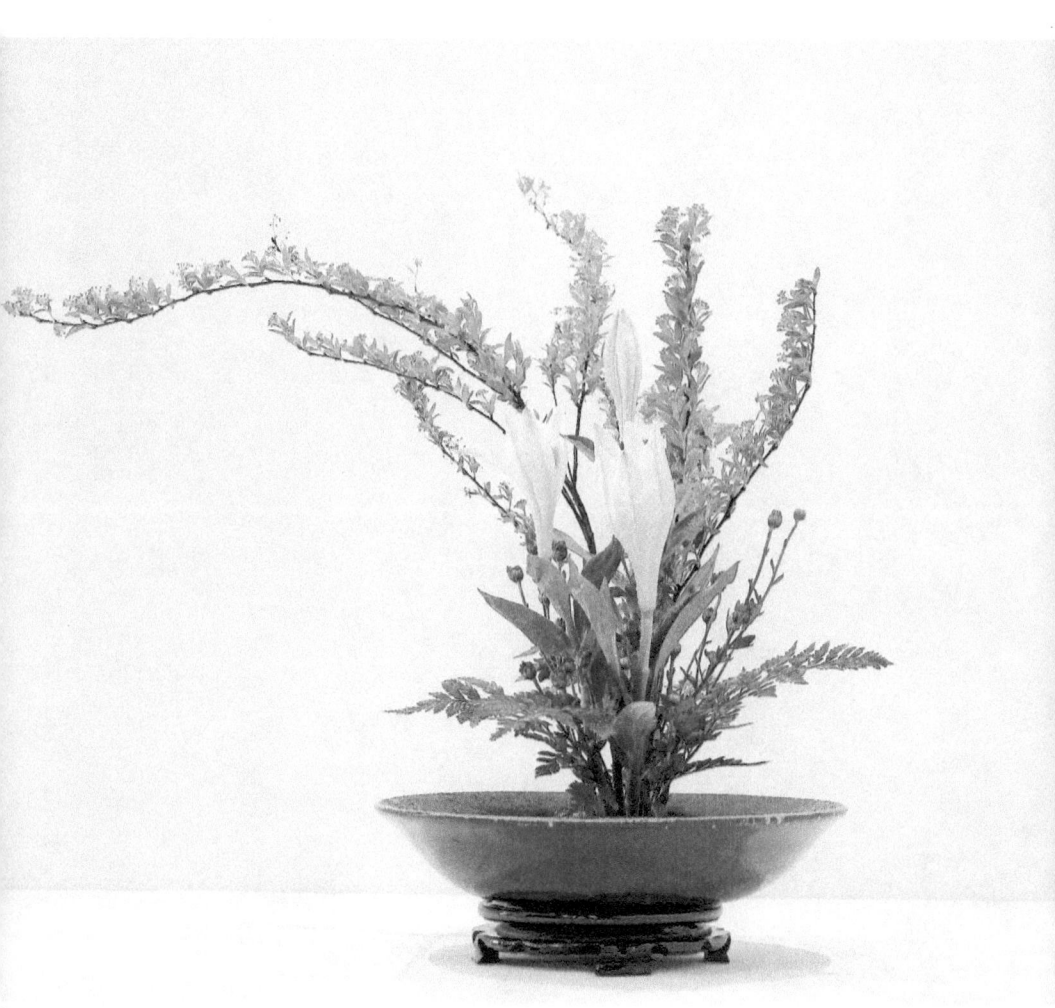